SAVING
TRUTH

CRASh PARAllEl

SAVING TRUTH

Finding Meaning & Clarity in a Post-Truth World

STUDY GUIDE

EIGHT SESSIONS

ABDU MURRAY

WITH BETH GRAYBILL

ZONDERVAN REFLECTIVE

Saving Truth Study Guide plus Streaming Video
Copyright © 2018 by Abdu H. Murray

This title is also available as a Zondervan ebook.

Published in Grand Rapids, Michigan, by Zondervan. Zondervan is a registered trademark of The Zondervan Corporation, L.L.C., a wholly owned subsidiary of HarperCollins Christian Publishing, Inc.

Requests for information should be addressed to customercare@harpercollins.com.

Zondervan titles may be purchased in bulk for educational, business, fundraising, or sales promotional use. For information, please email SpecialMarkets@Zondervan.com.

ISBN 978-0-310-17813-2 (softcover)
ISBN 978-0-310-09263-6 (ebook)

Published in association with Andrew Wolgemuth and the literary agency of Wolgemuth & Associates, Inc.

Cover design: Bruce Gore | Gore Studio, Inc.
Cover art: Shutterstock
Interior design: Kait Lamphere and Denise Froehlich

Printed in the United States of America
$PrintCode

Contents

OF NOTE

The quotations (unless otherwise indicated) interspersed throughout this study guide and the introductory comments are excerpted from the book, *Saving Truth: Finding Meaning and Clarity in a Post-Truth World,* and the video study of the same name by Abdu Murray. The reflection questions and between-session materials have been written by Beth Graybill in collaboration with Abdu Murray.

A Word from Abdu Murray

Hello, dear friend! This study guide and the eight video teaching sessions are a companion learning experience to be used with my book, *Saving Truth: Finding Meaning and Clarity in a Post-Truth World*. The pages of the book contain my personal thoughts and powerful facts based on years of research, excerpts from literature, and conversations with some of the most inquiring minds of our time.

The study guide and accompanying video study are designed to help you dig deeper into the topic of truth through personal reflection and biblical engagement, either as an individual or with a group. My goal is that you will come away with greater understanding of the post-truth mindset—of your neighbors, friends, colleagues at work, classmates, and acquaintances—as the world around you searches for meaning and clarity. I also pray that you will be more fully equipped to have thoughtful and grace-filled conversations about objective, biblical truth with these people God has placed in your life.

The purpose of the book and this study is more than just having you hear my personal thoughts on our post-truth culture. It is designed with three purposes in mind:

1. To help you understand the post-truth mindset and how it *infects* and *affects* us all as politicians and voters, pastors and philosophers, soccer moms and baseball dads, students and professors, creatives and scientists.
2. To equip you with facts and knowledge about the various areas of life where we are steeped in a post-truth mindset and losing our bearings as a culture, specifically: *our freedom, our humanity, our sexuality, faith and science,* and *religious pluralism*.
3. To explain how the message of Jesus can answer our deepest questions, and how the actions of Jesus can bring truth and clarity to a post-truth culture desperately in need of objective, biblical truth. The logical credibility of the Bible and the "inconvenient" truth of Jesus' message are the fixed point of reference we so desperately need.

I pray the Lord's blessing and understanding be upon you as you walk through this study, and as you represent and reflect his truth to the world around you. May God, our Lord and Savior, who is able to do immeasurably more than all we ask or imagine, work through you for his glory by spreading his joyous truth, which is salvation and eternal life for all who believe and follow Jesus. May he provide a solid foundation for the world and a fixed point of reference through you, my dear friend, as you reach out to those around you who are desperately in need of him. And may he give you the grace and confidence to be *in* the world and not *of* the world. I pray this in Jesus' name. Amen.

Abdu Murray

The Blossoming of the Culture of Confusion *and* The Church: Seductions of a Post-Truth Mindset

When everything is moving at once, nothing appears to be moving, as onboard ship. When everyone is moving towards depravity, no one seems to be moving. But if someone stops, he shows up the others who are rushing on, by acting as a fixed point.

Blaise Pascal

A fixed position allows us to get our bearings. If there are no fixed points of reference to regain clarity and clear up the confusion, we are left asking ourselves, "Are we going in the right direction? Are we moving backward or forward?" Our post-truth culture is awash in a sea of confusion. But there is One who stepped in the river of human history to provide an immovable fixed point of reference, even in the strongest of currents. I hope this study provides you with an understanding of the significance of Jesus' message and actions as our fixed point of reference for all truth, clarity, meaning, and direction.

INTRODUCTION

Riding on the Car Ferry

Some time ago I rode a car ferry across a river between Michigan and Ontario, Canada. Being from the Great Lakes state of Michigan, I'm used to the grand ferries that hold many cars. This ferry was not one of them. It held two cars at most, and that morning it was just me.

Because the ferry was so small and the trip so short, the deckhand asked me to stay in my car. I glanced down at my GPS just when the ferry pulled away from the dock, but I didn't see us leave nor did I feel the boat gently pull away. When I looked up from the GPS and my eyes met the flowing river, my body told me I was stationary, but my eyes told me that we were moving. Glancing at the ferry or the river didn't help because they were moving too. This was not like the typical bus-at-the-intersection incident where I could easily find a stationary, fixed point of reference to relieve the vertigo and clear up the confusion. There were no mailboxes or stoplights to use as a foundation or fixed point of reference. My dizziness and confusion persisted until I could see the unmoving land across the river.

Whenever we find ourselves in such situations, we instinctively try to end the disorientation by hurriedly locating a fixed point of reference. Culturally speaking, in the past decade we have found ourselves adrift in a wide river with no bearings in sight. We can barely see land's outline now, and we departed so long ago that we've forgotten what solid earth feels like. We have begun to question whether the land itself is anchored or afloat.

This is our post-truth culture awash in a sea of confusion. It is the post-truth mindset in which objective facts are less influential in shaping public opinions than our appeals to emotion and personal belief. We believe truth exists, but we don't care about truth if it gets in the way of our personal preferences. Our subjective feelings and opinions trump the truth, as do blatant falsehoods propagated to serve a higher political or social agenda.

I understand the struggle between preference and truth acutely as with those who embrace a post-truth mindset. For most of my life I was a proud Muslim. I thought Islam was the truest path to paradise, and every other worldview—especially Christianity—was wrong. But as I engaged with Christians about the claims of Christ, I had the discomfort of uncovering what former Vice President Al Gore might call "an inconvenient truth." History, logic, and science pointed to the credibility of the Bible in general and to the claims of Christ in particular. Coming to embrace and accept the truth about Jesus took me nine long years. The truth wasn't hard to find, but it was hard to embrace. Having listened to many voices and examined many worldviews, I'm convinced that Jesus' voice is the truest. The more post-truth spreads, the more desperately we need to know that Jesus can provide us with clarity and meaning.

As you begin this study of *Saving Truth: Finding Meaning and Clarity in a Post-Truth World*, it is first essential to understand the post-truth mindset of our current society and the Culture of Confusion it has created within the church. The post-truth culture is angry at Christians and rejects the message we carry. We must honestly assess our part in perpetuating the Culture of Confusion and fomenting the anger. This is necessary before we address the crucial questions of a post-truth culture, and before we look to the logical credibility of the Bible and the "inconvenient truth" of the message and actions of Jesus as the fixed point of reference for objective, biblical truth.

THINK ABOUT IT

What thoughts or questions come to your mind when you meet someone today who claims to be a Christian? How would you describe the cultural perspective of Christians today?

-or-

Consider a family member, friend, or some other person who has a negative perception of Christians or who is angry with the church. What does this person say about his or her frustration? How do they act? What kind of life do they live?

VIDEO TEACHING NOTES

The Blossoming of the Culture of Confusion

Questions we are asking in a post-truth culture:

- What does it mean to be human?
- Can we augment human reality?
- What does it mean to be male or female?
- What does sex mean?
- Is marriage a real institution?

Post-truth: The *Oxford English Dictionary's* 2016 Word of the Year

"A post-truth culture elevates feelings and preferences over facts and truth."

Two kinds of post-truth mentalities:
1. Soft mode: Truth exists, but we don't care
2. Hard mode: Truth exists, but I'm willingly going to lie to serve a higher agenda

Post-truth vs. postmodern

Post-truth and the scientific realm

"Here's the truth, no one is immune from the post-truth culture. A post-truth culture can infect us all."

Post-truth and the everyday realm

Seeds of the post-truth mindset: The Garden of Eden

"The Lord God took the man and put him in the Garden of Eden to work it and take care of it. And the Lord God commanded the man, 'You are free to eat from any tree in the garden; but you must not eat from the tree of the knowledge of good and evil, for when you eat from it you will certainly die.'"

Genesis 2:15–17 NIV

"The purpose of humanity was for a relationship with God."

Saplings of the post-truth mindset: Jesus and Pontius Pilate

"Everyone on the side of truth listens to me."

John 18:37 NIV

The single most important question today: What is truth?

The results of post-truth

Skepticism: The *skeptic* doesn't believe until there's enough evidence
Cynicism: The *cynic* doesn't believe even with the evidence

Full bloom of the post-truth mindset: Today's Culture of Confusion

"In today's post-truth culture, confusion is a virtue and clarity is a sin."

The post-truth mindset has infected every area of life:
- **Freedom**—What does true freedom mean?
- **Humanity**—What does it mean to be human, and what is human dignity?
- **Sexuality**—Have we elevated our preferences over truth?
- **Faith and Science**—Is faith antithetical to science?
- **Religious Pluralism**—Do all roads actually lead to God?

"As Christians, we can provide clarity about objective truth through the life of Jesus."

"Jesus answered, 'I am the way and the truth and the life. No one comes to the Father except through me.'"

John 14:6 NIV

The Culture of Confusion and the Church

Arabic saying: *Kulna fil hawa sawa* means "We're all in the same stink"

"The need to be on the 'right side' of things has caused the church to succumb to the temptation to be IN and OF the culture."

Who is the church?

- **Practicing Christians**—People who claim to be Christians as a way of life
- **Legacy Christians**—People who claim to be Christians as a cultural identity (per David Kinnaman and Gabe Lyons)

Two ways the church has given in to the post-truth mindset:

1. Avoiding conflict

"The post-truth mindset elevates feelings and preferences over truth and facts."

"Do not judge, or you too will be judged. For in the same way you judge others, you will be judged, and with the measure you use, it will be measured to you. Why do you look at the speck of sawdust in your brother's eye and pay no attention to the plank in your own eye? How can you say to your brother, 'Let me take the speck out of your eye,' when all the time there is a plank in your own eye? You hypocrite, first take the plank out of your own eye, and then you will see clearly to remove the speck from your brother's eye."

Matthew 7:1–5 NIV

"The 'new moral code' [so called by Kinnaman and Lyons] is the mindset that people should not criticize someone else's life choices."

2. Generating too much conflict

"People judge the quality of the message by the credibility and winsomeness of the messenger."

God's instructions: Love our enemies and be salt and light to the world

"But I tell you, love your enemies and pray for those who persecute you."

Matthew 5:44 NIV

"You are the salt of the earth. But if the salt loses its saltiness, how can it be made salty again? It is no longer good for anything, except to be thrown out and trampled underfoot. You are the light of the world. A town built on a hill cannot be hidden."

Matthew 5:13–14 NIV

Three ways to overcome the post-truth influence on the church:

    1. **Have a wise temperament**—The delivery of a message is just as important as the content

"Whoever restrains his words has knowledge, and he who has a cool spirit is a man of understanding."

Proverbs 17:27 ESV

"A fool gives full vent to his spirit, but a wise man quietly holds it back."

Proverbs 29:11 ESV

    2. **Use wise words**—Spread the whole truth

"It is better to remain silent and thought a fool than speak and remove all doubt."

Mark Twain

"The tongue of the wise commends knowledge, but the mouths of fools pour out folly."

Proverbs 15:2 ESV

"Our definition of sin doesn't come from comparison of others. It comes from God's standard of holiness. And our justification doesn't come with comparing ourselves with others, but rather from Christ's finished work on the cross."

Ed Stetzer

3. **Use wise actions: care for the culture**—Jesus included loving people along with loving God

"'Teacher, which is the great commandment in the Law?' And he said to him, 'You shall love the Lord your God with all your heart and with all your soul and with all your mind. This is the great and first commandment. And a second is like it: You shall love your neighbor as yourself. On these two commandments depend all the Law and the Prophets.'"

Matthew 22:36–40 ESV

"We must use a wise temperament, wise words, and wise actions if we are going to 'wear the coat of Jesus' well."

"Let your speech always be gracious, seasoned with salt, so that you may know how you ought to answer each person."

Colossians 4:6 ESV

VIDEO REFLECTIONS

1. Abdu is clear that the post-truth mindset has created a culture of confusion in our society. What effects of the post-truth mindset do you see in the world around you today?

2. As a Christian, where are you going for your information as you search for truth? If you're not a Christian, what are your perceptions about where Christians go for their sources of truth?

"Post-truth has two modes. The first is a 'soft' mode by which we may acknowledge that truth exists—or that certain things are true—but we don't care about the truth if it gets in the way of our personal preferences. Our subjective feelings and opinions matter more. The second is a 'hard' mode by which we exercise a willingness to propagate blatant falsehoods, knowing they're false, because doing so serves a higher political or social agenda."

3. The post-truth culture elevates feelings and preference over facts and truth. Has there ever been a time in your own life when you've allowed your personal feelings and preferences to override facts and truth? What was the situation or circumstance?

4. Have you ever stopped to consider how your biases and motivations are influencing your search for truth? What are some of these biases for you, or what are the motivating factors that tempt you to choose preferences over facts?

"The creep of post-truth is seen in how we gather information about the world to conform to what we want to be true, not to what is actually true. In fact, research shows that many of us get our news from comedy and satire shows, not from time-tested news sources. Viewers watch these shows, satisfied by the parody of 'the other side' of an issue, while fooling themselves into thinking they are being informed. You can still be a fan of these shows, but be careful not to lose perspective on the facts and truth."

Read: Genesis 2–3; John 18:37; John 14:6

5. As Christians, what does it mean to be *in* the culture but not *of* the culture? What kind of challenge does this concept pose for you personally?

"When we label people, then the church begins to look just like the culture."

"Who is the church? When the broader culture thinks of the church, they lump everyone who claims to be Christian into one batch. But David Kinnaman and Gabe Lyons differentiate between two different kinds of Christians. Legacy Christians use Christianity as a cultural identity in the background noise of their lives. Practicing Christians see Christianity as a way of life, as a guiding sense of spiritual direction."

6. According to Kinnaman and Lyons' definitions (see page 19), what kind of Christian are you? What would the people closest to you say, or what would the people in your everyday life say?

7. Abdu says when we succumb to the post-truth culture, we risk betraying the very truth that we claim to champion and our claims to follow Jesus who embodies truth. What do you think about this statement? How have you witnessed this kind of betrayal of the truth in the American church?

Read: Matthew 7:1–5; Matthew 5:44; Matthew 5:13–14; Proverbs 17:27; Proverbs 29:11

8. The church has contributed to the Culture of Confusion and the post-truth mindset by (1) *avoiding conflict* and (2) *generating too much conflict*. Can you give examples of how the church has responded to conflict in each of these ways?

9. Abdu highlights how we often misuse Scripture to avoid the truth. What are some of the common Scriptures you hear frequently misused in our current post-truth church culture?

Read: Proverbs 12:23; Proverbs 15:2; Matthew 22:36–40; Colossians 4:6

"If you are a practicing Christian, it's important to take a deep, sobering look at just how we may have contributed to the culture's confused state. As Christians, we too have succumbed to the post-truth mindset similar to the way the rest of the culture has. Or we use the truths of Scripture to bludgeon outsiders. We create 'us versus them.'"

10. Recall the story of Jakob and Cimmerman from the video teaching. Cimmerman told Jakob, "I have given my life to the Lord because you wear his coat well." In today's culture, how can we be a church that wears the coat of Jesus well?

11. How might this journey drive you more into prayer, the Bible, seeking truth, and greater love for Jesus and the church? What are one or two steps you can take to seek and understand truth over your own preferences and biases?

CLOSING PRAYER PROMPTS

- Ask God to help you, and the Christians you know, understand the post-truth mindset.
- Ask God to help the church acknowledge the ways we have all contributed to the Culture of Confusion with the absence of conflict or too much conflict.
- Invite the Holy Spirit to give you the courage to live with a humble, proper sense of judgment as we see in Matthew 7:1–5.

- Pray for the people in your life who are seeking meaning, clarity, and direction. Ask God to help them know the truth of the Bible, love God, and walk closely with Jesus.
- Pray for peace and confidence in your own heart as you trust Jesus to guide you and our culture out of post-truth and into truth.

"When the church has doubled down on its commitment to truth, especially in the face of opposition, it has flourished, brought credibility to the gospel and benefitted society. For Christians, now is the time for compassionate, yet uncompromisingly expressed, truth. If the church's caving to the post-truth mindset has contributed to the larger cultural problem, then perhaps Christians' rediscovered commitment to the truth can lead us back to the solution."

Between Sessions

PERSONAL REFLECTION

Take time to think and journal about the following questions.

What are the signs or symptoms of the Culture of Confusion and a post-truth mindset in your own life or in the lives of the people closest to you?

Do you believe in objective truth? Why or why not? How do you balance your preferences and biases with the truth?

Who in your world is cynical or skeptical? How can you tell? How does this study session encourage you to change your actions or your conversational approach with that person?

How can you wear the coat of Jesus well as an individual? How can you encourage your fellow Christians and your local church community to wear the coat of Jesus well?

What changes do you hope for in your friends, family, work or school or neighborhood community, or local church outreach as you practice this mindset?

PERSONAL PRAYER JOURNEY

Use a separate journal or the space provided here.

- Begin journaling your prayers to God as you take a personal look at how you have participated in the post-truth seductions by making the gospel pill easier to swallow in order to avoid uncomfortable discussions with non-Christians. How do you handle difficult Bible passages that challenge their behavior preferences?
- Write prayers of confession expressing the ways you participated in post-truth seductions by using the truths of Scripture to criticize or socially "bludgeon" non-Christians. How have you contributed to the "us-versus-them" mentality?

"Often as Christians we make church so unwelcoming that we repel the very people who could benefit from what Jesus has to offer. But love has historically motivated Christians. Paul Lee Tan expressed that 'a Christian is a mind through which Christ thinks, a heart through which Christ loves, a mouth through which Christ speaks, a hand through which Christ helps.'"

DIGGING DEEPER

Exploring the Seeds of Post-Truth

Take time to study the seeds of post-truth from the earliest days of our existence in Eden and beyond. As you read the passages, use the space provided to collect your insights and thoughts.

Read: Genesis 2:4–25 and 3:1–13

Insights about the post-truth mindset of Adam and Eve as they interact with Satan in the Garden of Eden:

Read: John 18:28–40

Insights about the post-truth mindset of Pontius Pilate as he interacts with Jesus during Jesus' betrayal and arrest:

The Antidote to Post-Truth

Read: Matthew 7:1–5

Insights about Jesus' example of judging another person's actions:

"It's worth pausing for a moment to see just how Jesus' words actually express a message opposite to what so many want him to have expressed. Jesus says that when we remove the log from our own eye, we will see clearly how to judge our brother's actions. In the full context, we see that Jesus is saying that when we judge, it is to be for the improvement of others, not their condemnation."

Read: Titus 3:1–11

Insights about the apostle Paul's expectations of the way we live our lives as Christians:

"Fair or not, people judge the credibility of a message by the integrity of the messenger. If the gospel message of compassion, forgiveness, and reconciliation is proclaimed by those who seem to have none of those qualities, it's hard to see how the broader culture's response can be anything but . . . dismay and anger."

Read: Matthew 22:34–40

Insights about loving God and loving others:

Exploring Great Resources

- Abdu tells the story of Jakob and Cimmerman from Marie Chapin's book *Of Who the World Was Not Worthy*. Consider reading the full story about Jakob, a missionary from the former Yugoslavia, and Cimmerman, a farmer who lost much due to the country's rampant violence and corruption.
- The book of Proverbs provides a template for how Christians can once again be as savory as salt and illuminating as light in a bitter and dark time. Consider reading one Proverb a day for one month.

- Watch *The Passion of the Christ* (2004) to get a secondhand perspective on the conversation between Jesus and Pontius Pilate.
- Over the past years many excellent online resources have emerged that can help you grow in your faith, understand our culture, and learn to help others walk toward Jesus. Some of the best online resources are the website for Ravi Zacharias International Ministries (rzim.org) and the ministry's YouTube channel. You will find excellent videos, articles, and more. Take time to explore those sites and review the resources that are just a click away.

People Matter

Our words are so important. Words are meant to convey truth and bring life, not peddle falsehood or foster pain. If Christians are God's ambassadors, then we are called to carefully choose our words. So, we must ask ourselves: *Do our words convey truth? Do they convey life?* We are often tempted to answer questions and controversies of our day, but the issues don't need an answer; people do.

"Let your speech always be gracious, seasoned with salt, so that you may know how you ought to answer each person."

Colossians 4:6 ESV

DEEPER LEARNING

As you reflect on what God is teaching you through this session, you may want to read chapters 1 and 2 of the book *Saving Truth: Finding Meaning and Clarity in a Post-Truth World* by Abdu Murray. In preparation for your next session, you might want to read chapter 3 of the book.

JOURNAL, REFLECTIONS, AND NOTES

Soft Truth / Hard Truth

Bema Podcast

Confusion's Consequences— Getting Freedom Wrong

In a post-truth culture, where preferences and opinions are elevated over facts and truth, anything that challenges our preferences, even if a challenge is laced with facts, is deemed offensive and oppressive. This current climate has arisen because we have mistaken autonomy for freedom. We need to understand the foundations for freedom itself because freedom has become a confused concept today. Freedom becomes chaotic in a system without constraints, and operates at its best within the confines of truth.

INTRODUCTION

The Ironic Sacrifice

We are losing our freedom in the quest for autonomy in our post-truth culture. A great example of this is what's happening these days on college campuses, where the powers that be have revoked or attempted to revoke the approved status of Christian groups because these groups restrict their leadership (*not membership*) to Christians. In other words, they are being penalized for being Christian.

But it isn't just Christians who feel the pressure. Well-known atheist Richard Dawkins was disinvited from a radio station in Berkeley, California, due to his critiques of Islam. University professors of every political bent are being attacked, shouted down, or branded as racists for not catering to student sensibilities.

In another arena, California legislators passed a bill making it punishable by a fine for a long-term care facility or anyone working there to "willfully and repeatedly fail to use a resident's preferred name or pronouns after being clearly informed of the preferred name or pronouns." If someone is a biological male but asks you to call him a woman, the state will punish you if you refuse to do so. In other words, the state will take away your freedom if you fail to bow to someone else's autonomy.

We no longer just elevate personal preferences over truth. We elevate our particular preferences over the preferences of others. Only *my* preferences matter. Reason dies in the quest for autonomy. This quest is like heading down an endless road with no traffic lights or painted lines. And as we hitchhike along that road, we may jump into a car that's going partly our way, only to kick out the driver after he's served our purpose.

This pursuit of autonomy also drives increasingly ferocious attacks against the Bible as the standard for truth and conduct. Many people oppose the Scriptures as an outmoded method of control that arbitrarily suppresses human behavior. This stems from the failure to see differences between unfettered individual autonomy and true freedom. They are not the same.

Confusing freedom with autonomy has enslaved our rational minds and our moral senses. And soon it may enslave us altogether. We need to know the truth that our quest for autonomy is what enslaves us. We are in chains that we cannot feel and in prisons we cannot see.

THINK ABOUT IT

What does *freedom* mean to you? How would your colleagues, friends, classmates, or family describe *freedom*? If you have a differing perspective than the people around you, why do you think that is?

-or-

Have you ever unknowingly or unwillingly offended someone because you didn't understand their preferences? What was that experience like for you? How did the other person respond to you?

VIDEO TEACHING NOTES

Freedom: Is it really the ability to do whatever we want?

Autonomy: In Greek is *autos*, "self," and *nomos*, "law," which translated means we are a law unto ourselves

Freedom requires boundaries *to truly be free*

The problem with autonomy: My law vs. your law
- Truth can no longer be the arbiter
- Power is the only deciding factor between us

"We have sacrificed truth and clarity on important issues on the altar of preferences and human autonomy."

Three consequences of sacrificing truth:

1. We lose our ability to reason
   - University of Missouri (2005)—*freedom of speech*
   - Yale University (2015)—*freedom of expression*
   - Gender Identity—*freedom of gender fluidity*

"Our quest for autonomy makes some facts undeniable, but it makes our autonomy undebatable."

   - Inconsistent use of the term *identify*

2. We lose our sense of moral accountability
   - Man is everything

"Man is the measure of all things."

Protagoras

Secular humanism maintains that "through a price of value inquiry informed by scientific and reflective thought, men and women can reach rough agreement concerning values, crafting ethical systems that deliver optimal results for human beings in a broad spectrum of circumstances."

Tom Flynn

   - Self-deification

"To be men, we must be in control. That is the first and last ethical word."

Joseph Fletcher

"We no longer feel ourselves to be guests in someone else's home and therefore obliged to make our behavior conform with a set of pre-existing cosmic rules. It is our creation now. We make the rules. . . . We are responsible to nothing outside ourselves, for we are the kingdom, the power, and the glory forever and ever."

Jeremy Rifkin

When we sacrifice clarity and truth on the altar of autonomy, we are accountable to no one but ourselves.

"Go wiser thou! And, in thy scale of sense
Weigh thy opinion against Providence;
Call imperfection what thou fanciest such,
Say, here he gives too little, there too much;
Destroy all creatures for thy sport or gust,
Yet cry, if man's unhappy, God's unjust;
If man alone engross not Heav'n's highest care,
Alone made perfect here, immortal there;
Snatch from his hand the balance and the rod,
Rejudge his justice, be the god of God.
In pride, in reasoning pride, our error lies;
All quit their sphere, and rush into the skies.
Pride still is aiming at the blest abodes,
Men would be angels, angels would be gods.
Aspiring to be gods, if angels fell,
Aspiring to be angels, men rebel;
And who but wishes to invert the laws
Of order, sins against th' Eternal Cause."

Alexander Pope

"When we give up being made in God's image—the Imago Dei—so that we can be god ourselves, we no longer have a higher moral value."

3. We lose our sense of human value
   - Peter Singer—The value of human life

"We have taken on God's job of ascribing value to certain people because we have become gods in our own image . . . but we are horribly unqualified for God's job!"

"We are more powerful than ever before but we have no idea what to do with all that power. Worse still, humans seem to be more irresponsible than ever. Self-made gods with only the laws of physics to keep us company, we are accountable to no one. We are consequently wreaking havoc on our fellow animals and on the surrounding ecosystem, seeking little more than our own comfort and amusement, yet never finding satisfaction. Is there anything more dangerous than dissatisfied and irresponsible gods who don't know what they want?"

Yuval Noah Hurari

The ironic sacrifice

"We have sacrificed clarity and truth about who we are and what our purpose is on the altar of autonomy and have made ourselves God."

We lose freedom in the quest for autonomy

Authoritarianism: "Men and women of steel will lift us out of this muck"

"Voices and activities across the spectra are being silenced because they suggest there are limits to our autonomy."

The Bible addresses autonomy

In those days there was no king in Israel. Everyone did what was right in his own eyes.

Judges 17:6 ESV

Jesus claims to be the source of truth

"So Jesus said to the Jews who had believed him, 'If you abide in my word, you are truly my disciples, and you will know the truth, and the truth will set you free.' They answered him, 'We are offspring of Abraham and have never been enslaved to anyone. How is it that you say, 'You will become free'?'"

John 8:31–33 ESV

When we value autonomy over everything else, this distorts our view of reality. When truth is no longer our guide, preferences matter more.

There is a better way forward

VIDEO REFLECTIONS

1. What comes to mind when you think of the word *lawless*? Have you ever experienced a state of "lawlessness"? If so, what was that like?

2. After hearing the differences between *freedom* and *autonomy* from Abdu's perspective, what comes to your mind? What new thoughts or questions, or even past memories, do you associate with this distinction between freedom and autonomy?

"The great thing about facts and data is that when they disprove something, you can't—or shouldn't—ignore it. That's how progress happens. The United States has risen to the most powerful and prosperous nation in human history based on facts, an educational system that taught them, a legal system that respected them, and a political system that made it all possible."

3. Abdu listed three consequences of sacrificing truth. Can you think of recent examples from current events to illustrate these consequences?
   - We lose our ability to reason.
   - We lose our sense of moral accountability.
   - We lose our sense of human value.

4. Which one of these three consequences have you been most influenced or affected by? How so?

5. How have we lost our freedom to the rise of autonomy as a society? And as Christians, how have we been silenced? Share some practical examples from your own life experiences.

"Here we are now, in a world where practically anything is permissible except the idea that some things shouldn't be."

Read: Genesis 1:27; Genesis 5:1; Psalm 8:5

6. Abdu reminds us of our human value as we bear the Imago Dei—the image of God. What does it mean to be made in God's image?

Read: Judges 17:6; Judges 18:1; Judges 19:1; Judges 21:25

7. When we deal with our leaders today, whether we think they are good or bad or somewhere in the middle, do we do it with truth as our guide? How do we see ourselves in today's autonomous culture—as men and women of truth and authority, humility and obedience, *or* as tolerant bystanders afraid of offending someone or being called out?

"These people failed to remember they had been enslaved to Egypt for 400 years! In fact, so confused was their thinking that they forgot that they were under Roman occupation at the very moment they claimed not to be enslaved by anyone."

Read: John 8:31–47

8. What similarities do you see between the Jews of Jesus' day and the people of our day? How did Jesus respond to the Jews? How do you think Jesus would respond to our post-truth mindset today?

"What I'm advocating for each one of us, individually in our hearts, is to search once again for the source of true freedom. It will be no surprise that I believe that God provides us with true freedoms that come from clarifying the confusion that has saturated the culture and blinded us from seeing who and what we were intended to be."

CLOSING PRAYER PROMPTS

- Thank God for giving his Word, the Bible, to lead and guide us with his truth, and thank God for being Truth.
- Confess where you need to grow in your understanding of freedom and release the autonomous chains of tolerance and preference.
- Ask God for discipline to exercise your ability to reason, to maintain a sense of moral accountability, and to continue valuing human life.
- Pray for deep and genuine humility when you talk with people who have questions about truth or strong opinions about their preferences.
- Invite God to bring more people into your life and sphere of influence who need his truth and freedom.

Between Sessions

PERSONAL REFLECTION

Take time to think and journal about the following questions.

How can you be confident that Jesus is the way, the truth, and the life?

How has the Bible helped to shape your perspective on truth as a foundation for your daily life?

As you prepare to stand for truth as reflected in Jesus' messages and actions, what current topics do you need to understand in greater depth? What resources will you use and when will you do this research?

PERSONAL PRAYER JOURNEY

Use a separate journal or the space provided here.

- Begin journaling your prayers to God as you take a personal look at how you have been tempted to sacrifice the truth in these ways: *your ability to reason, your sense of moral accountability,* and *your sense of human value.* Ask God to help you see where you've succumbed to false truths in these areas, and ask him to help you walk in truth, obedience, and humility moving forward.

DIGGING DEEPER

Take time to understand the consequences of confusion and how we have gotten freedom wrong as a post-truth culture. Consider the passages beginning on page 41 and how they will help you grow in your faith. Use the space provided to collect your insights and thoughts.

"The Old Testament book of Judges tells us of Israel's rejection of freedom and quest for autonomy, a desire to have no authority above themselves. Everyone did what was right in their own eyes. In other words, they pursued personal preferences over truth. Each time the people's thirst for autonomy landed them in trouble, God sent a judge—a person who took his authority from God—to guide the people. But they rejected God's authority time and again in favor of their personal sovereignty until the resultant chaos became too much. Eventually the people cried out for a human king. As the Bible puts it, this was a rejection not of the judges and prophets who had guided Israel, but of God himself as the determiner of what is good and valuable."

Israel Gets a King

Read: 1 Samuel 8:1–22

Insights about Israel's requests for a king:

How this insight shapes my faith:

"This is the essence of unfettered human autonomy—to become as God but without the benefit of divine wisdom. We have become gods unaccountable to anyone or anything. And the problem is that we are utterly unqualified for God's job. We are more powerful than ever before but have very little idea of what to do with all that power."

The Imago Dei

Read: Psalm 8

Insight about being created in God's image:

How this insight shapes my faith:

Abiding in Jesus

Read: John 8:31–47

 Insight about Jesus:

 How this insight shapes my faith:

Read: John 14:5–14

 Insight about Jesus:

 How this insight shapes my faith:

Read: John 14:15–21

 Insight about Jesus:

 How this insight shapes my faith:

Read: John 18:37

Insight about Jesus:

How this insight shapes my faith:

A Life of Truth

Read: Psalm 86:11–13

Insight about living a righteous life:

How this insight shapes my faith:

Addressing Sinful Humanity

At some point, we must recognize our own sinful humanity and the fact that seeing ourselves as determiners of truth—seeing ourselves as gods—is, in reality, idolatry. Romans 1:20–25 illustrates sinful humanity.

Take time to read these verses and write out three or four insights on what it means to be sinful humanity:

-
-
-
-

It is our responsibility, as Christians in a post-truth culture, to address the sinful humanity in our own hearts as well as the hearts of others, graciously. Write out three to four insights you gained from this lesson on addressing the consequences of sinful humanity:

-
-
-
-

Pray for opportunities to clear up confusion for the people in your life by shedding truth and light on the questions and preferences.

DEEPER LEARNING

As you reflect on what God is teaching you through this session, you may want to read chapter 3 of the book *Saving Truth: Finding Meaning and Clarity in a Post-Truth World* by Abdu Murray. In preparation for your next session, you might want to read chapter 4 of the book.

JOURNAL, REFLECTIONS, AND NOTES

_____

_____

_____

_____

_____

_____

_____

_____

_____

_____

_____

_____

_____

_____

_____

Clarity about Freedom

The paradox was that when I thought I was most free, responsible and reasonable, I was least. I was a slave to my own desires and to the spirits that drove them. Real freedom is something altogether different—it starts on the inside. As martyrs and the persecuted have testified, we can have real freedom inside a prison wall.

Mary Poplin

INTRODUCTION

Freedom's Foundation

Think of all the movies whose central theme is freedom. From *Braveheart* to *The Patriot*, from *Saving Private Ryan* to *Amistad* and *Glory*, our stories focus on the human struggle to win freedom or to keep someone else from taking it away.

America's founding was a daring attempt to institute a government that acknowledged and encouraged freedom. The Declaration of Independence tells us that every person has inalienable rights to life, liberty, and the pursuit of happiness. By definition, a right is inalienable because no person or group of people (like the government or society) can take it away. When someone is enslaved, his or her right to liberty isn't taken away even though it is violated.

Regimes that have rejected God and viewed freedom as a creation of the state have historically oppressed human freedom and rights—from Stalinist Russia to nationally socialist Germany, from communist China to Kim Jong-un's North Korea. Inalienable rights, therefore, must be grounded in a source beyond human authority. In this way, their existence doesn't depend on human opinion, reasoning, or behavior. If they did, inalienable rights simply wouldn't exist. And if inalienable rights don't exist, then America itself is an illusion. Even some of those among us with allegiance to atheistic naturalism agree that without God, freedom itself is an illusion.

But reliance on a document like the Declaration of Independence or the U.S. Constitution isn't enough. Those are just the century-old statements of men in powdered wigs, after all. A declaration based merely on human preferences scrawled in pen across parchment paper is just as flimsy. But if it's founded on something—better yet, *someone*—that transcends time, space, matter, and opinions, then the rights and freedoms it declares have transcendent substance.

Freedom becomes clear when we recognize that God is freedom's unchanging source. And Jesus—history's most influential person—expressly binds freedom to the limits of truth. He gently tells us that truth is freedom's foundation; truth is the wall that protects freedom from the invasion of chaotic autonomy.

Freedom to pursue the truth comes only when we recognize that there is an objective truth out there for us to freely pursue. According to Jesus, truth and freedom are always linked. Any attempt to separate them diminishes our ability to enjoy either. Our recognition that there are objective truths to be discovered leads to the freedom to discover them. In turn, our discoveries foster greater freedom to pursue more truths.

But our post-truth Culture of Confusion has attempted to derail this cycle of truth and freedom by inserting the preferences of autonomy. So, let's unpack just how applicable Jesus' two-thousand-year-old words are to our current cultural confusion and our desperate need to clarify the nature of freedom.

THINK ABOUT IT

Now that you understand the difference between autonomy and freedom, I'm going to ask you again: *What does freedom mean to you?* What adjectives or other words would you use to describe freedom? (Take note: It's interesting to hear the words we each use to describe freedom because it may mean different things or evoke different feelings for different people.)

-or-

Briefly share about a time when you experienced the upside of freedom and a time when you experienced the downside of freedom. What did you learn from those experiences?

VIDEO TEACHING NOTES

Understanding freedom provides clarity

"So, Jesus said to the Jews who had believed him, 'If you abide in my word, you are truly my disciples, and you will know the truth, and the truth will set you free.' They answered him, 'We are offspring of Abraham and have never been enslaved to anyone. How is it that you say, "You will become free"?' Jesus answered them, 'Truly, truly, I say to you, everyone who practices sin is a slave to sin. The slave does not remain in the house forever; the son remains forever. So if the Son sets you free, you will be free indeed.'"

John 8:31–36 ESV

Know the truth, *then* it sets you free. Truth is necessary for freedom.

Autonomy has no limits. Truth has necessary boundaries. Thus, freedom has limits.

"Freedom sounds simple, straightforward and self-evident. . . . But freedom is both more complex and more contested than many realize, so those who would guard freedom with care must regard freedom with respect."

Os Guinness, A Free People's Suicide

Two aspects of freedom:
- **Negative freedom**—*freedom from*—the freedom from interference and constraint (Isaiah Berlin)
- **Positive freedom**—*freedom for*—freedom for excellence according to whatever vision and ideals define that excellence

"By itself, negative freedom looks like autonomy."

Objective truth: To have an ideal we must have objective truth
- Objective truth is critical to freedom
- Jesus binds freedom and truth together
- The post-truth culture idolizes negative freedom

The shift: "Do whatever you want" to "Be whatever you want"
- Possibilities with positive freedom
- Consequences with negative freedom

"In the day-to-day trenches of adult life, there is actually no such thing as atheism. There is no such thing as not worshipping. Everybody worships. The only choice we get is what to worship. And the compelling reason for maybe choosing some sort of god or spiritual-type thing to worship—be it JC or Allah, be it YHWH or the Wiccan Mother Goddess, or the Four Noble Truths, as some inviolable set of ethical principles—is that pretty much anything else you worship will eat you alive. If you worship money and things—if they are where you tap real meaning in life—then you will never have enough, never feel you have enough. It's the truth. Worship your body and beauty and sexual allure and you will always feel ugly. And when time and age start showing, you will die a million deaths before they finally plant you. On one level, we all know this stuff already. It's been codified as myths, proverbs, clichés, epigrams, parables; the skeleton of every great story. The whole trick is keeping the truth up front in daily consciousness. Worship power—you will end up feeling weak and afraid, and you will need ever more power over others to numb you to your own fear. Worship your intellect, being seen as smart—you will end up feeling stupid, a fraud, always on the verge of being found out."

David Foster Wallace

Moral truth is the boundary of freedom

"The only restraint that does not contradict freedom is self-restraint."

Os Guinness

Backyard boundaries: We've lost our purpose when we lose our restraint

"Art is limitation; the essence of every picture is the frame. If you draw a giraffe, you must draw him with a long neck. If, in your bold creative way, you hold yourself free to draw a giraffe with a short neck, you will really find that you are not free to draw a giraffe. The moment you step into the world of facts, you step into a world of limits. You can free things from alien or accidental laws, but not from the laws of their own nature. You may, if you like, free a tiger from his bars; but do not free him from his stripes. Do not free a camel of the burden of his hump: you may be freeing him from being a camel."

G. K. Chesterton

Ultimate devaluing: We're trying to free ourselves from ourselves

Freedom and the Bible

"For you were called to freedom, brothers. Only do not use your freedom as an opportunity for the flesh, but through love serve one another. For the whole law is fulfilled in one word: 'You shall love your neighbor as yourself.' But if you bite and devour one another, watch out that you are not consumed by one another."

Galatians 5:13–15 ESV

"What we worship might eat us alive."

David Foster Wallace

"We must not eat each other with our own freedom."

The foundation of freedom in God
- Inalienable right: a right that cannot be taken away
- The power to grant rights is also the power to take away
- Inalienable rights must come from beyond humanity

A syllogism
The inalienable right to freedom exists only if God exists.
The inalienable right to freedom does exist.
Therefore, God exists.

Free people

"True freedom exists only if God exists. He acts as both the source of and the restraint on our freedom."

"Jesus answered them, 'Truly, truly, I say to you, everyone who practices sin is a slave to sin. The slave does not remain in the house forever; the son remains forever. So if the Son sets you free, you will be free indeed.'"

John 8:34–36 ESV

The proof of Jesus as truth: His resurrection*
C: Crucifixion's historical evidence
A: Appearances to disciples
S: Skeptics converted
E: Empty tomb

---

* Abdu Murray's debate with atheist John Loftis, "Was Jesus Raised from the Dead?" can be found on https://youtu.be/66E-OykI9UY.

The resurrection and freedom

"We were intended to be in communion with God, and the historical reality of the resurrection makes that possible."

The freedom equation

**Freedom from restraint + Freedom for the greater good + Freedom from sin
= Freedom for what we were meant to be, free indeed**

"When we have a full understanding of freedom, we can treat others with dignity."

VIDEO REFLECTIONS

1. Let's go back to Abdu's story about his children playing in the backyard. Have you ever had to create boundaries for your children, your friends, your teammates, or your colleagues in order to protect them and actually allow for more freedom? What was the situation, and how did they respond?

"How remarkable is it that God, knowing us, has established the boundaries of freedom that keep us from running blindly into traffic, childishly chasing after the bouncing ball of our liberty."

Read: John 8:31–36

2. How have we been enslaved by sin as a culture, and how have we been set free by the truth? How about for you *personally*—how have you been enslaved by sin, and how have you personally been set free by the truth?

Read: Galatians 5:13–15

3. When was the last time you exercised your freedom by looking out for the best interests of others? What did you have to sacrifice personally in order to serve others in that way?

"Paul tells us about the need to self-restrain our negative freedom so that we can act in each other's best interests, which is positive freedom. If we worship freedom in the service of self-gratification, we will end up devouring each other."

4. Abdu makes the distinction between *positive freedom* and *negative freedom*. How have you experienced positive freedom—*freedom for*? Or negative freedom—*freedom from*?

"Contrary to contemporary belief, the Bible doesn't set up arbitrary boundaries to oppose our freedom. Its boundaries favor our fulfillment. The Bible, in which God tells each one of us about our uniqueness and value, stands against the stealthy enslavement that comes from a muddled, one-sided view of freedom."

Freedom Explained in the Bible

In its very structure, the Bible describes freedom in all its aspects, from winning it to structuring it to maintaining it.

- **The Four Gospels:** In these books—written by Matthew, Mark, Luke, and John—Jesus wins our freedom through his life, death, and resurrection.
- **The Book of Acts:** The disciples wrestle with Old Testament law and newfound freedom in Jesus' fulfillment of the law.
- **The Doctrinal Books of the New Testament:** In these books—written by Paul, Peter, James, Jude, John, and others—we learn how to practice and sustain our freedom.

Read: Matthew 27:11–26

5. Considering the two kinds of freedom, what kind of freedom was Pontius Pilate exercising here? How do you think Pilate felt about the decision he made standing before the crowd that day?

"The hard reality is that for most people, unbounded freedom results in emotional and spiritual enslavement."

Read: Acts 2:22–24

6. How did the death and resurrection of Jesus redefine freedom for the early church in the New Testament? How does your conviction that Jesus died on the cross and rose again move you to share truth with confidence and boldness today?

7. What do we lose as individuals and as a society when we focus on *freedom from*? What do we gain when we focus on *freedom for*?

"Mere freedom from restraint doesn't encourage us to engage in the great quests to better society or to help others. . . . It encourages a sort of narcissistic preoccupation on the self and the fulfillment of our private desires."

Read: Galatians 2:15–21

8. We have true freedom because Jesus won that freedom for us on the cross. So then, our freedom is actually Jesus' freedom to exercise in us and through us. How can we bring both perspectives on freedom—*positive* and *negative* freedom—to our post-truth culture as we wear the coat of Jesus well in the world around us?

"Whenever humanity has coupled our love of negative freedom to our need for positive freedom, tremendous public good has resulted. This must not be ignored. Positive freedom to pursue true ideals gave birth to the great movements that restored negative freedom to the disenfranchised and abused."

CLOSING PRAYER PROMPTS

- Thank Jesus for his willingness to die for your freedom.
- Give God praise for the glory of the resurrection. Acknowledge that the resurrection of Jesus is real and is also the key to your salvation and to the validity of truth.
- Ask God to deepen your faith and strengthen your love for Jesus as you learn more about Jesus as the foundation of truth and freedom.
- Ask God to deepen your understanding of these concepts of *positive* freedom and *negative* freedom so you can live them out as you love and serve others.
- Thank God for inherent dignity in your own human existence and the existence of those around you as a result of true freedom found in Jesus.

"Jesus rose from the dead, and someone who rises from the dead has credibility. That's what makes the gospel so unique among religious and nonreligious messages claiming to offer us freedom. The gospel is rooted not in ideologies or ideas, but in identity—specifically Jesus' identity. Jesus doesn't tell us that an abstract concept like "the truth" will set us free. He makes the truth tangible and personal by telling us that he, the Son, will set us free."

Between Sessions

PERSONAL REFLECTION

Take time to think and journal about the following questions.

The resurrection of Jesus is the key to finding meaning and clarity in our post-truth world. Are you convinced of the resurrection of Jesus? If you have questions or struggles with this, what are they? How can you overcome these points of doubt?

If Jesus won our freedom, and you put your faith and trust in him, what holds you back from walking in true freedom? Are there specific areas of your life where you get stuck or easily stumble with exercising freedom?

"A clearer understanding of freedom allows us to act with the sacredness of other human beings in mind, and we can only be sacred beings if our value comes from God."

Where or how are you currently exercising negative freedom—*from*—something or someone? Where or how are you currently exercising positive freedom—*for*—something or someone?

How are you using these freedoms to love and serve others? If these are areas of growth, make a list of steps you will take to start exercising these freedoms.

PERSONAL PRAYER JOURNEY

Use a separate journal or the space provided here.

- Journal prayers for friends who need truth and freedom. Pray and ask God to show you how you can use your freedom *for* the good of others.

DIGGING DEEPER

Understanding the Resurrection Story in the Gospels
Read the closing sections of the Gospels and write down everything you learn about the death of Jesus and his resurrection.

Read: Matthew 26–28

Insights about the death of Jesus:

Insights about the resurrection of Jesus:

Read: Mark 14–16

Insights about the death of Jesus:

Insights about the resurrection of Jesus:

Read: Luke 22–24

Insights about the death of Jesus:

Insights about the resurrection of Jesus:

Read: John 18–21

Insights about the death of Jesus:

Insights about the resurrection of Jesus:

Now take a few moments to reflect on the central themes from all four Gospels about the death and resurrection of Jesus. What stands out to you? What lessons have you learned?

The Benefits of Freedom

Reflect on your life and consider ways you've benefited from freedom. Identify some of the ways others have exercised freedom on your behalf. Make a list that includes global freedoms as well as specific freedoms you enjoy because of the sacrifice and passion of others.

The Positive Freedoms I Enjoy

Globally:

-
-
-
-

Personally:

-
-
-
-

The Negative Freedoms I Enjoy

Globally:

-
-
-
-

Personally:

-
-
-
-

DEEPER LEARNING

As you reflect on what God is teaching you through this session, you may want to read chapter 4 of the book *Saving Truth: Finding Meaning and Clarity in a Post-Truth World*. In preparation for your next session, you might want to read chapter 5 of the book.

JOURNAL, REFLECTIONS, AND NOTES

Clarity about Human Dignity

In the Culture of Confusion where nothing seems anchored and uncertainty is lauded as virtue, we have to ask ourselves if we have any way to get back on track toward restoring a clear vision for the common good. Or will the fissures of confusion and uncertainty cause the mosaic of our hopes to further crumble?

INTRODUCTION

The Golden Rule

At the United Nations headquarters in New York is a stone mosaic based on a painting by the famous American artist Norman Rockwell. With Rockwell's characteristic detail and soft tones, the mosaic depicts people from different ethnic, racial, and religious backgrounds standing in solidarity. It's at once an eye-catching and heartwarming piece of art.

Inscribed in the mosaic are the words, "Do Unto Others As You Would Have Them Do Unto You"—what has come to be known worldwide as the Golden Rule. The mosaic has become one of the U.N. headquarters' most popular attractions.

The Golden Rule mosaic had cracked and deteriorated over time, needing restoration. How strangely poetic. As our culture's moral framework has crumbled, our understanding of the essence of human dignity has likewise cracked.

The restored *Golden Rule* mosaic was unveiled at a rededication ceremony during which U.N. Deputy Secretary-General Jan Eliasson explained its importance. "It reflects the very essence of our mission as set out in our Charter," he said. "At its core, the work is about narrowing the gap between the world as it is and the world as we want it to be." I think Eliasson was saying that the U.N.'s work, at least in intention, is to narrow the gap between the fractured, violent world we see and the peaceful, human-dignifying world we wish we lived in.

The Golden Rule, as inscribed on the U.N. mosaic, is easily one of the most quoted and recognized idioms in human history. Yet we seldom realize who first uttered those words in that particular way. It was, of course, Jesus of Nazareth who said, "So in everything, *do to others what you would have them do to you*, for this sums up the Law and the Prophets (Matthew 7:12 NIV, emphasis mine). This sentiment is also expressed in other religious and nonreligious traditions—with subtle yet important differences—including Hinduism, Buddhism, Islam, and Unitarian Humanism. All of these religious and nonreligious versions express the common belief that we should demonstrate the value and dignity of other humans by our actions. And yet we've veered far from that common belief.

Our common understanding of human dignity has fractured. We've become tribal. Those with whom we agree have dignity; everyone else is a hate-filled adversary. We've lost sight of the fundamental definition of what it means to be human, and we've forgotten that we need each other to fit into a unified, designed mosaic. So let's revisit the message of this iconic mosaic and discover what Jesus truly meant by the Golden Rule.

THINK ABOUT IT

Have you ever viewed *The Golden Rule* mosaic at the United Nations headquarters in New York? If so, what was the experience like for you? Or if you've viewed another powerful piece of symbolic artwork, describe that experience's effect on you.

-or-

What does the Golden Rule mean to you? How has it been used in the past to guide your attitude and your actions? Or how does it inspire you today?

VIDEO TEACHING NOTES

The Golden Rule

The Mosaic "reflects the very essence of our mission as set out in our Charter. At its core, the work is about narrowing the gap between the world as it is and the world as we want it to be."

Jan Eliasson, United Nations Deputy Secretary-General

"So in everything, do to others what you would have them do to you, for this sums up the Law and the Prophets."

Matthew 7:12 NIV

An interfaith perspective of the Golden Rule:
- **Hinduism:** "This is the sum of duty; do not do to others what would cause pain if done to you." Mahabharata 5:1517
- **Buddhism:** "Hurt not others in ways that you yourself would find hurtful." Udana-Varga 5:18
- **Islam:** "None of you [truly] believes until he wishes for his brother what he wishes for himself." Number 13 of Imam Al-Nawawi's "Forty Hadiths"

- **Unitarian Humanism:** "We affirm and promote respect for the interdependent web of all existence of which we are a part."

The common belief in human dignity

The confusion: Unprecedented uncertainty about human identity *(Does being human really mean anything?)*

Secular humanism: Humans are special, but we don't need God to justify it

"The underlying ethical principle of Planetary Humanism is the need to respect the dignity and worth of all persons in the world community. . . . We affirm that moral values derive their source from human experience. Ethics is autonomous and situational, needing no theological or ideological sanction. Ethics stems from human need and interest. To deny this distorts the whole basis of life. Human life has meaning because we create and develop for our futures."

Paul Kurtz

The commonality to affirm human dignity

The autonomy that we claim gives us dignity undermines our dignity

"Gone is purpose; all that is left is direction. This is the bleakness we have to accept as we peer deeply and dispassionately into the heart of the Universe."

Peter Atkins

"People are monkeys with large brains. Period."

Richard Posner

Key question: What gets you up in the morning?

Naturalism does not explain the human mind (per Tallis and Nagle)

The secular confusion: We are equal to God but less than human

"What we need is clarity that comes from an objective understanding of what we are as humans, and who God is—the objective value giver."

The gospel clarity: We are less than God but more than machines

"What is man that you are mindful of him, and the son of man that you care for him?"
King David, Psalm 8:4 ESV

The Bible: It is quite clear that we are glorious but shame ridden

The human heart

"The heart is deceitful above all things, and desperately sick; who can understand it?"

Jeremiah 17:9 ESV

"For out of the heart come evil thoughts, murder, adultery, sexual immorality, theft, false witness, slander."

Matthew 15:19 ESV

Made in God's image

"Then God said, 'Let us make man in our image, after our likeness. And let them have dominion over the fish of the sea and over the birds of the heavens and over the livestock and over all the earth and over every creeping thing that creeps on the earth.'"

Genesis 1:26 ESV

"He answered, 'Have you not read that he who created them from the beginning made them male and female . . .?'"

Matthew 19:4 ESV

"God didn't just come to say something about the human condition; he came to *do* something about the human condition because you and I are objectively valuable."

The cross and our confusion: The cross is where human depravity and human dignity collide

When I survey the wondrous cross
On which the Prince of Glory died,
My richest gain I count but loss,
And pour contempt on all my pride.

Forbid it, Lord, that I should boast,
Save in the death of Christ my God!
All the vain things that charm me most,
I sacrifice them to His blood.

See from His head, His hands, His feet,
Sorry and love flow mingled down!
Did e'er such love and sorrow meet,
Or thorns compose so rich a crown?

Isaac Watts, "When I Survey the Wondrous Cross"

God defines relationship and love

"Anyone who does not love does not know God, because God is love."

1 John 4:8 ESV

To be fully human

The incarnation of Jesus

"For even the Son of Man came not to be served but to serve, and to give his life as a ransom for many."

Mark 10:45 ESV

The resurrected state of Jesus

"On the evening of that day, the first day of the week, the doors being locked where the disciples were for fear of the Jews, Jesus came and stood among them and said to them, 'Peace be with you.'"

John 20:19 ESV

The resurrection and human dignity

"When we are glorified, we have more weight than the rest of the world."

C. S. Lewis, The Weight of Glory

"Until I opened my life to Christ, I, like the general secular academic community, absolutely hated the idea of sin; even hearing the word *sin* was like scratching nails on a board, and hearing the name of Jesus was even more disconcerting. Now I see that the solution to sin—the simple cleansing—is one of the most brilliant, hopeful and freeing principles of Judeo-Christianity."

Mary Poplin

The application

"The gospel is not just relevant to you, but you are relevant to God."

The root of true human dignity

The Golden Rule: Their interpretation vs. Jesus' interpretation

"How can we see each other as broken beings worth sacrificing for because Jesus sacrificed for us?"

VIDEO REFLECTIONS

1. What stood out to you in this session? Is there a question you have as a result of what you learned? Or is there something that inspired you, encouraged you, or changed your perspective on human dignity?

"Everyone, regardless of beliefs, orientations, and preferences, has inherent dignity and intrinsic value."

Read: Matthew 7:12

2. Describe a time when you were mindful of the Golden Rule and how this mindfulness changed the outcome of a situation or conversation.

Read: Matthew 7:24–28

3. Jesus uses a metaphor in this passage to describe those who hear his words and respond to them, and those who hear his words and choose *not* to respond. Which person do you relate to the most? Why?

"And so the first thing we should note is the common desire among the religious and nonreligious to affirm human dignity. Yet at the heart of secular attempts to affirm objective human dignity lies a confused coherence."

4. Abdu establishes that it is "the common desire among the religious and nonreligious to affirm human dignity." What role have you played personally and collectively in affirming human dignity? If this has not been the norm for you, what steps could you take to personally and collectively affirm human dignity?

"There is a growing recognition of this confusion among secular thinkers, and some are unflinchingly trying to clarify matters by denying that humans have objective value and dignity. According to such voices, we are either just chemically sophisticated machines or evolutionarily gifted animals."

5. Consider the various perspectives of human value and dignity: some people believe we are just chemically sophisticated machines, while others believe we are evolutionarily gifted animals. In which circles or arenas of society do you think these beliefs tend to be more common? How have you responded to people who have expressed one of these perspectives to you?

"If human beings are reduced to machines or animals, there really is no nobility to anything we do because the recipients of our seemingly noble acts aren't really noble either. And yet, we can't seem to help thinking that we do have intrinsic dignity and that our professional pursuits are noble."

Read: Jeremiah 17:9; Matthew 15:19

6. The Old Testament prophet Jeremiah declared the human heart "deceitful" and "sick." Jesus echoed similar words when he described the "evil" that comes out of the human heart. Even the Qur'an acknowledges that human morality is worthy of destructive judgment (Sura 35:45). Most of humanity agrees we have a heart problem, so why do you think we resist the truth that we need to be redeemed by a source outside of ourselves? Why do we have a hard time embracing the reality of human sin?

"An impressive body of scientific evidence demonstrates that the mind is not the brain and that human mental activity survives brain death. Our human intentionality is not a naturally occurring phenomenon. It is something put into us by a designer."

Read: Genesis 1:26; Matthew 19:4

7. If we embrace the reality of human sin, how can we be made in the image of God? What does it look like to be image-bearers of God considering the disparity of the sinful human heart?

"Our dignity and hope for redemption lies in God made flesh, the God who took on human form to rescue humanity from itself. The cross is where human depravity and human dignity collide."

Read: Psalm 139

8. Consider this: our moral choices affect God himself because of his love for us. God's love for us is what gives us our human dignity. How does this perspective change your view of God? How does this perspective change the way you ascribe and express dignity to the people around you?

CLOSING PRAYER PROMPTS

- Thank Jesus for the gift of human dignity, and for the clarity God provides in his Word.
- Give God praise for the gravity of the cross which is the ultimate demonstration of our dignity. Acknowledge that this gift is not just a gift for all of humanity; it is a personal gift to *you*.
- Ask God to deepen your understanding of the paradox of human dignity and the depravity of our sin.
- Ask God to show you what it means to live in the fullness of our human dignity—a dignity that brings meaning to our endeavors and aspirations.
- Thank God for the opportunity to wear the coat of Jesus well by living out the Golden Rule: "do to others as we would have them do to us." This is the ultimate expression of his love for humanity.

"The gospel tells us that we are not merely physical beings. Nor are we ethereal beings. We are a functional unity of body and soul. Both are important. Both have dignity. It is through God—the transcendent ground of all being—that we have our being."

Between Sessions

PERSONAL REFLECTION

Take time to think and journal about the following questions.

"In John 20, we see Thomas and the rest of the disciples hiding in a locked room following Jesus' crucifixion. In that room, Thomas heard the eyewitness testimony of his comrades that Jesus was raised bodily from the grave. But he remained skeptical. He needed to see Jesus' living body and feel the nail scars and wounded side before he'd believe. It was at that moment that Jesus walked *through* the door, even though his resurrection body was physical. After the resurrection, his body was both physical and glorified—it was weighty."

How are you like Thomas—skeptical, unsure, confused? Where do you still need clarity regarding the idea of human dignity?

What does the idea of *weighted glory* mean to you? As a follower of Jesus, how or where do you sense the *weighted glory* of your life?

"C. S. Lewis observed that good is original and evil is merely a perversion, 'that good should be the tree and evil the ivy . . . that good should be able to exist on its own while evil requires the good on which it is parasitic.' This means that there is hope for us despite our parasitic sin. It means that we can be redeemed and our intended purpose can be restored."

How has your life been redeemed by trusting in Jesus? What do you think it means for our intended purpose to be restored? How does this redemption and restoration influence the contribution you bring to creating clarity in the world?

PERSONAL PRAYER JOURNEY

Use a separate journal or the space provided here.

- Journal prayers for friends who need to understand their dignity and worth. Pray and ask God to show you how you can use your clarity and understanding about human dignity to encourage them.

DIGGING DEEPER

Understanding the Glory of God and Humanity

Take time to understand how the glory of God provides clarity to our questions regarding human dignity. Consider the passages below and how they will help you grow in your faith. Use the space provided to collect your insights and thoughts.

Read: John 20

Insight about Jesus' resurrected glory:

How this insight shapes my faith:

Read: 1 Corinthians 15:42–49

Insights about our resurrected glory:

How this insight shapes my faith:

Read: Acts 17:24–28

Insights about our human dignity from God:

How this insight shapes my faith:

Read: Ephesians 2:10

Insights about our human dignity from God:

How this insight shapes my faith:

Addressing Human Dignity

"As humans, we ascribe a pragmatic social contract theory to the Golden Rule: We refrain from doing bad things so that bad things won't be done to us. We treat others well so that they won't hurt us. But Jesus' wording is subtly, yet profoundly, different. By saying, 'Do to others what you would have them do to you,' Jesus tells us to treat others well *even if they never treat us well*."

The pragmatic contract theory promotes the idea of self-preservation. Can you think of one or two examples of self-preservation in your own life? And one or two examples from our post-truth culture?

- •
- •
- •
- •

But Jesus promotes the idea of self-sacrifice. Can you think of one or two examples of self-sacrifice in your own life (your sacrifice or the sacrifice others have made for you)? And one or two examples from our post-truth culture?

-
-
-
-

Pray for opportunities to show the self-sacrificial love of Jesus as you encourage clarity, meaning, and dignity to our post-truth world.

DEEPER LEARNING

As you reflect on what God is teaching you through this session, you may want to read chapter 5 of the book *Saving Truth: Finding Meaning and Clarity in a Post-Truth World*. In preparation for your next session, you might want to read chapter 6 of the book.

JOURNAL, REFLECTIONS, AND NOTES

_____

_____

_____

_____

_____

_____

_____

_____

_____

_____

_____

_____

_____

_____

_____

Clarity about Sexuality, Gender, and Identity

The topics of sexuality and gender identity are by far clouded in the most confusion and emotion. Sexuality is a powerful part of the human experience. It not only pertains to our physical pleasure but also to our emotional well-being. It has a mysterious gravitational tug on our identities. The same is true of gender identity. That's why anger and misunderstanding are such potent factors that keep real conversation from happening. We just try to understand each other and why our differences exist as the necessary first step toward clarity.

INTRODUCTION

Strangely Common Ground

I've never been confused about my sexual preferences or gender. Yet something about another person's struggle for identity resonates with me. Perhaps it's because eighteen years ago, so much about me suddenly changed. For the twenty-seven years prior, I was a proud Muslim, sure that Islam as a religion and Muslims as a community had the answers to life's questions. I shared those answers with non-Muslim friends and invited them to be open-minded about Islam.

But when the credibility of classical Christianity confronted me, the gospel I once derided as nonsense looked more credible by the day. And that gospel was telling me something very different about who I am, who God is, what life is about, and where salvation lies. The more solid Christianity's ground became, the more seasick I felt. I simply didn't *want* Christianity to be the fixed point of reference by which my world—especially my identity—was measured.

For most of my nine-year search, my identity was simply too much to risk. But as the near decade-long sojourn brought me within an oar's length of the gospel's shoreline, I was beckoned to embrace the gospel no matter the cost. In those last months and weeks, I could hear Jesus, in the voice I imagined him to have, repeating, "Everyone who is of the truth listens to my voice" (John 18:37 ESV). Despite the cost, I eventually responded to that voice.

Perhaps that's why the continuing debate over sexual and gender identity stalks my mind and heart. Perhaps that's why I'm sensitive to the turmoil behind the eyes of those who are in the midst of the sexual or gender identity tug-of-war. My journey isn't identical to someone who is trying to understand his or her same-sex attractions or gender identity. Yet we may have the common ground of a painful search from which to explore where clarity can be found.

The Culture of Confusion's growing obsession with autonomy fuels a movement that encourages us to individually define sexual and gender identity. An agenda that pushes for total autonomy breezes past the deep efforts of those with ingrained but unwanted dysphoria or same-sex attraction. And this "autonomy above all else" mentality causes some to rage against the Bible as a repressive tool created by prejudiced, heterosexual, and male-dominated cultures. Unfortunately, some in today's church haven't helped much to change that perception.

If anything, it's the Bible, even with its limitations on sexual expression, that is pro-love and pro-people. This statement is undoubtedly difficult for many to believe. So let's keep exploring the post-truth topic of cultural confusion as we look at sexuality, gender, and identity.

THINK ABOUT IT

Is there someone in your life experiencing confusion about their sexuality, gender, or identity? What is it like for you to watch them deal with this confusion? What words would you use to describe their journey? If this is you, what words would you use to describe your own journey?

-or-

Have you ever comforted or counseled someone dealing with sexuality, gender, or identity confusion? What words or passages of Scripture brought the most understanding and comfort to their circumstances or to the situation?

VIDEO TEACHING NOTES

Sexuality, gender, identity, and dignity

The air of understanding: Does Christianity have anything to offer when it comes to sexuality?

Not understood. We move along asunder:
Our paths grow wider as the seasons creep
Along the years; we marvel and we wonder
Why life is life, and then we fall asleep—
Not understood.

Not understood. How many breasts are aching
For lack of sympathy. Ah, day by day,
How many cheerless, lonely hearts are breaking.
How many noble spirits pass away—
Not understood.

cont.

O God! that men would see a little clearer,
Or judge less harshly when they cannot see!
Oh God! that men would draw a little nearer
To one another! They'd be nearer Thee,
And understood.

Thomas Bracken, "Not Understood"

The cultural terrain

"The boundaries of sexual expression are broadening and confusion no longer equals confusion anymore; it now means something different."

Common ground

Uncommon ground

"We no longer see people; we only see controversies."

"We believe it is indispensable to deconstruct the binary sex/gender system that shapes the Western world so absolutely that in most cases it goes unnoticed. For 'other sexualities to be possible' it is indispensable and urgent that we stop governing ourselves by the absurd notion that only two possible body types exist, male and female, with only two genders inextricably linked to them, man and woman. We make trans and intersex issues our priority because their presence, activism and theoretical contributions show us the path to a new paradigm that will allow as many bodies, sexualities and identities to exist as those living in this world might wish to have, with each one of them respective, desired, celebrated."

The International Gay and Lesbian Human Rights Commission

Autonomy vs. human welfare

The church: In favor of institution or in favor of people?
- Find a common moral foundation
- Ask questions about objective morality—*is anything wrong with anything?*
- Understand a theistic worldview—*there is only morality if God exists*

All of us are broken

"Clearing a browser history isn't the same thing as clearing a conscience because the windows of our souls are our eyes and they are covered in grime, and we need the Holy Spirit to clean those windows."

Us vs. Them mentality

"Even humble Christians who make every effort to be kind and gracious toward homosexuals are not really reaching OUT; they're reaching DOWN from a place of moral elevation."

Jenell Williams Paris, The End of Sexual Identity

"If homosexuality binds us to sin, heterosexuality blinds us to sin."

Michael Hannon

Holy sexuality (Christopher Yuan)

Understanding sexuality: The Bible as a foundation
- Atheism and Humanism

"We are machines for propagating DNA."

Richard Dawkins

- Pantheism (including Hinduism)
- Islam
- Christianity

The Bible as the objective standard: Why does the Bible say what it says about homosexuality?

The sacred beauty of sexuality: What is sacred about our sexuality?
  1. We are all made in the image of God
  2. Sex within the bond of marriage allows us to reflect the divine

"Now Adam knew Eve his wife, and she conceived and bore Cain, saying, 'I have gotten a man with the help of the LORD.'"

Genesis 4:1 ESV

"A man shall leave his father and his mother and hold fast to his wife, and they shall become one flesh."

Genesis 2:24 ESV

"Have you not read that he who created them from the beginning made them male and female, and said, 'Therefore a man shall leave his father and his mother and hold fast to his wife, and the two shall become one flesh?' So they are no longer two but one flesh."

Matthew 19:4–6 ESV

  3. Unity and diversity reflected in marriage: *echad* (Hebrew) means "unified"

Clarity about gender identity

"No one is satisfied with anyone else's perspective on the topic of gender identity."

Mark Yarhouse

Gender Terms

Transgender—biologically one sex, but who thinks of themselves as another

Transsexual—identifies as a sex different than their biological sex

Cisgender—someone whose gender identity matches their biology

Gender Fluid—someone who wants to be flexible about gender identity

Gender Dysphoria—distress with the incongruence of identity and biology

---

"Only about 0.005 and 0.014 percent of adult males and between 0.002 and 0.003 percent of adult females have gender dysphoria. Other studies suggest that the prevalence of gender dysphoria is between 1 in 10,000 to 1 in 13,000 males and 1 in 20,000 to 1 in 34,000 females."

Gender dysphoria and autonomy

Gender dysphoria and the church

"I don't think you chose to experience your gender incongruence."

Mark Yarhouse

The church needs to allow people to see a true sense of community and identity

---

The Traditional Church Model (per Yarhouse)

Current: Behave → Believe → Belong
Ideal: Belong → Believe → Become

A New Model

Believe (see value) → Belong (see the better God has for them)
→ Become (become who God intended them to be)

The renewal of our minds

"But I say, walk by the Spirit, and you will not gratify the desires of the flesh."

Galatians 5:16 ESV

Struggling and suffering: Finding solace in our identity in Christ

"Suffering in Christianity is not only not meaningless, it is ultimately one of the most powerful media for the transmission of meaning. We can stand in adoration before the cross, and kneel and kiss the wood that bore the body of our Savior, because this is the means by which the ugly meaningless atheistic suffering of the world (the problem of evil) was transmuted into the living water, the blood of Christ, the wellspring of creation. The great paradox here is that the tree of death and suffering is the tree of life. This central paradox in Christianity allows us to love our own brokenness precisely because it is through that brokenness that we image the broken body of our God—and the highest expression of divine love. That God in some sense wills it to be so seems evident in Gethsemane: Christ prays, 'Not my will, but thine be done,' and when God's will is done it involves the scourge and the nails. It has also always struck me as particularly fitting and beautiful that when Christ is resurrected, his body is not returned to a state of perfection, as the body of Adam in Eden, but rather it still bears the marks of his suffering and death—and indeed it is precisely through these markers that he is known by Thomas."

Melinda Selmys

John 5: Jesus heals the paralyzed man

"If we understand and stand for biblical truth and affirm the dignity of the person, perhaps Jesus can use us to help people who are struggling."

VIDEO REFLECTIONS

1. There are a lot of conversations in our Culture of Confusion about what it means to love as Christians. Based on what you learned today, what do you think it means to love the people around us going through sexual, gender, and identity confusion? If this is you, how do you want to be loved?

"The trouble with truth is that it demands something of us. It demands that we yield our desires and desired identities to God's providence and sovereignty."

2. Is there a question you have as a result of what you learned in this session? Is there something that inspired you, encouraged you, or changed your perspective regarding the way we, as Christians, engage our post-truth culture as a whole?

"When Christians think of others as more broken than them, they flirt with an unbalanced view of biblical sexuality and the sinfulness of humanity. So many Christians seem to forget their own brokenness in self-righteously judging those with same-sex attractions."

Read: Galatians 5:16–26

3. Whether we wrestle with our sexuality or not, we have all wrestled with our identity at some point in our lives. Considering the quote at the bottom of page 91, what desires and desired identities have you had to yield to God in this season of life? How are you walking by the Spirit as you yield these desires?

"Acknowledging same-sex sex as sinful expresses nothing more, but nothing less, than this: all of us are fractured in every way, including but not limited to our sexuality. We're broken in different ways, but we are broken together. Together we need restoration."

Read: Romans 1:25; 1 Corinthians 6:7–11

4. Name some ways we show dishonor as a culture. What kind of effect has this dishonor had on our society? Think about someone you know whose life has been restored from dishonor after finding their true identity in Christ. What inspires you about their transformation?

"When we get clarity on *why* the Bible says what it does, we can get clarity on *who* the Bible says we are. God isn't arbitrarily prohibiting certain conduct; he is protecting something sacred."

Read: Ephesians 5:21–33; Revelation 19:7–9; Revelation 21:1–7

5. The New Testament refers to the church as the "bride of Christ." What does this mean according to Scripture? How does the church as a whole reflect this description? How does your local church reflect the "bride of Christ"?

Read: Genesis 1:27; Genesis 2:24; Matthew 19:4–6

6. Scripture talks about marriage between a man and woman as "becoming one." Scripture also talks about God as one being with three distinct and divine personhoods (the Trinity). How does marriage between a man and woman reflect the unity and diversity of God as it relates to the Trinity of God?

"If we understand and stand for biblical truth and affirm the dignity of the person, perhaps Jesus can use us to help people who are struggling."

Read John 5:1–15

7. What stands out to you in the story of the paralyzed man? How did Jesus help the man who was struggling? Who else may have been struggling in this story? How did Jesus help them?

8. Abdu suggested that the church become a place where people can *believe*, then *belong*, then *become*. What action steps will you take as part of the local church to help those struggling with identity confusion to *believe* their value, *belong* by seeing the better God has for them, and *become* who God has intended them to be?

CLOSING PRAYER PROMPTS

- Thank Jesus for the gift of our true identity found in him.
- Give God praise for clarity provided in the Bible regarding the truth and redemption of our identities as men and women made in his image.
- Ask God to deepen your understanding of our human sexuality, gender identity, and biblical truth. And ask God to show you the areas of your life where you too need healing and restoration.
- Ask God to show you what it means to create a place in the church where people who are struggling, confused, and broken can find a safe place to wrestle with their questions and find community.
- Thank God for the opportunity to express his love and objective truth to the world around you. And thank God for the ability to increase your understanding, expand your capacity to listen, and step into the wisdom he freely gives to all who follow him.

"For whoever would save his life will lose it, but whoever loses his life for my sake will find it."

Matthew 16:25 ESV

Between Sessions

PERSONAL REFLECTION

Take time to think and journal about the following questions.

"Many of us have a hard time resisting fast food or giving up bad habits for our own good or to honor God. But thousands of people submit their deepest desires to Christ not just on a daily basis, but on a moment-by-moment basis. How many of us, whether Christian or not, can say that we've had such constancy of devotion to anything or anyone?"

What habit(s) do you need to give up? Which actions or choices have been dishonoring to you, to God, and to the human dignity he's given to you? Highlight a habit you're going to address and the necessary steps you will take to stop it.

Earthly relationships are not our savior. God himself is our Savior. How have you placed savior-like expectations on your marriage or your relationships? What thoughts or expectations do you need to remove from a spouse or relationship and give back to God? What does it look like for you to allow God to be your Savior?

"The church needs to open its doors and Christians need to open their hearts so that those struggling to find resolution to their [gender] dysphoria—and those who are struggling to find clarity amidst other confusions—can find community and, ultimately, their true identity in Christ. In Christ, they can be understood."

How can you be a part of the solution when it comes to the local church providing community and a safe place for struggling, confused individuals who need to understand their true identity in Christ?

PERSONAL PRAYER JOURNEY

Use a separate journal or the space provided here.

- Journal prayers for friends who need clarity regarding their identity in Christ. And pray for your heart and for the Christians in your community who need to open themselves to a posture of love and understanding.

DIGGING DEEPER

Understanding the Gender Identity of God

Take time to understand how God represents the truth of our identities through the expression of binary genders in Scripture. Consider the passages below and how they will help you grow in your faith. Use the space provided to collect your insights and thoughts.

"We are given the privilege through opposite-sex marriage to reflect the unity in diversity of God, who is the foundation of reality. From this we can begin to see that God-ordained sexuality and marriage secure the importance and dignity of established binary genders. God refers to himself in masculine pronouns and labels: he is God the Father, God the Son, King of Kings, and so on. But he also self-refers in feminine aspects."

Read: Matthew 23:37

Insights about the feminine aspects of God:

How this insight shapes the way I live out my faith or my perspective on how others live out their faith:

Read: Luke 13:34

Insights about the feminine aspects of God:

How this insight shapes the way I live out my faith or my perspective on how others live out their faith:

Read: Deuteronomy 32:18

Insights about the feminine aspects of God:

How this insight shapes the way I live out my faith or my perspective on how others live out their faith:

Read: Isaiah 66:13

Insights about the feminine aspects of God:

How this insight shapes the way I live out my faith or my perspective on how others live out their faith:

Addressing the Confusion

"When Christians mistake genuine [gender] dysphoria for willful rebellion, the mistreatment comes in the form of either unwarranted judgment or exclusion from the church—the one place where people should be able to find their true identity in Christ. When the autonomy-obsessed among us view gender as a matter of choice, the mistreatment takes the form of minimizing (or even trivializing) the real anguish those with dysphoria go through."

In what specific ways have you judged or been judged regarding this topic of confusion regarding sexuality and gender identity?

Who do you need to offer forgiveness or receive forgiveness from in regard to your answers to the previous question? Name specific people that come to mind and take a moment to pray for those people. Ask God to give you the freedom to forgive and the courage to ask for forgiveness. If you sense God asking you to give forgiveness or ask for forgiveness in person, make it a point to follow through out of love and obedience to God.

Pray for opportunities to show the love of Jesus as you encourage clarity and community for people who are struggling, confused, and broken in regard to their humanity and their God-given identity.

DEEPER LEARNING

As you reflect on what God is teaching you through this session, you may want to read chapter 6 of the book *Saving Truth: Finding Meaning and Clarity in a Post-Truth World*. In preparation for your next session, you might want to read chapter 7 of the book.

JOURNAL, REFLECTIONS, AND NOTES

Clarity about Science and Faith

There is confusion today about how science and faith interact, and this confusion creates false narratives of opposition. While we often credit science with the world's wonderful advancements, we blame religion for all of society's ills. However, religion is more like science than some might wish to acknowledge. While usually including rules and commands, religion is also a method for making sense of the world. And many religions, like Christianity, embrace science as a means to understand the natural part of the larger reality while also embracing philosophy, theology, and other means of exploring the nonphysical parts of reality.

THE GREAT FILTER

INTRODUCTION

The Search for Harmony

Through science we have made wonderful discoveries like penicillin, tectonic plates, and planetary bodies. We've invented airplanes, cars, and even the computer I'm typing on. But we need more than naturalistic sciences. We cannot derive meaning, human value, and equality from a laboratory.

Science intentionally focuses on the universe's mechanistic workings. Thus, limiting ourselves to sciences forces us to look at the wider panorama of reality through a narrow keyhole. Science can help us see aspects of the physical world that were once unseen. But if we only look at the world through science's filter, we will rob ourselves of the broader view.

And hard sciences aren't broad enough to help us unlock all of life's mysteries. We need history to learn lessons about our past failures and successes. Literature and poetry inspire us and make us self-reflective. Philosophy helps us explore logic. Good religion takes all of those fields and combines them with revelation to tell us who we are, why we're here, and where we're going. Confusion comes when we claim that science is the sole means of understanding the world. And clarity comes when we acknowledge the transcendent.

The fact is, everyone has a faith of some kind. Without it, life would be unlivable. If we acted based only on absolute certainty of knowledge, we could never actually do anything. When you drive to work, you don't test your brakes to make certain that they won't fail and plunge you into a fiery car wreck. You trust the brakes. But that trust isn't blind. You have enough evidence that brakes tend not to fail without warning to warrant getting into your car without going through a multi-point inspection.

Although science is a limited tool by which we explore the natural or physical world, what we learn through science has implications for our understanding of the supernatural. In other words, science, when used as a tool in the search for truth, can reveal signals of transcendence—hints in life that point us to God. Science can actually lead us to see that we are significant and relevant not only to each other but also to the One who created it all. Science confirms the truths in Scripture. Scripture unveils the poetry of science.

So here it is, the harmonious overlay of science and faith. We come to know things through our senses and by applying our reasoning and wisdom. We have faith based on what we know, however incomplete our knowledge may be. While seemingly contradictory, faith and science are mutually complementary. Together, they give us a clearer picture of the simplicity and complexity of the world around us.

THINK ABOUT IT

How have you explored and explained the relationship between science and faith? What are your most pressing questions when it comes to the relationship between science and faith?

-or-

How does your faith shape your perspective on science? How does your experience with science shape your perspective on faith?

VIDEO TEACHING NOTES

Clarity about science and faith

"A delusion is a persistent false belief held in the face of strong contradictory evidence, especially as a symptom of psychiatric disorder. . . . God is . . . a delusion and a pernicious delusion. . . . When one person suffers from a delusion, it is called insanity. When many people suffer from a delusion it is called religion."

Richard Dawkins, The God Delusion

"Science flies you to the moon. Religion flies you into buildings."

Victor Stenger

The historical conflict between science and faith

"To get past the confusion to clarity, we have to figure out what science cannot tell us."

What science cannot tell us

"Science is the study of the natural world; the study of cause-and-effect relationships of the natural and the physical world."

The limitations and self-defeating beliefs of science
- Scientism

"If nothing else, the attack on traditional religious thought marks the consolidation in our time of science as the single system of belief in which rational men and women might place their faith, and if not their faith, then certainly their devotion. From cosmology to biology, its narratives have become *the* narratives. They are, these narratives, immensely seductive, so much so that looking at them with innocent eyes requires a very deliberate act. And like any militant church, this one places a familiar demand before all others: Thou shalt have no other gods before me."

David Berlinski

- We are just machines

- Science and the purpose of humanity

"We are just a bit of pollution. . . . If you got rid of us, and all the stars and all the galaxies and all the planets and all the aliens and everybody, then the universe would be largely the same. We're completely irrelevant."

Lawrence Krauss

- Science and morality

- Science and racial equality

"Science can inform a conscience, but it can't create one."

Science and faith

"We have to understand the limits and scope of science. And we have to understand the definition of faith if we are to understand the interaction of faith and science. Faith is not belief without knowledge or in the face of strong contradictory evidence."

"Now faith is the substance of things hoped for, the evidence of things not seen."

Hebrews 11:1 KJV

"Now faith is the assurance of things hoped for, the conviction of things not seen."

Hebrews 11:1 ESV

The Greek word for faith is *pistis*, which literally translated means "trust"

"Everyone has faith, but is the object of our faith worthy?"

"Atheism requires as much faith as theism." Reason and faith are "two dimensions of one truth; they are interdependent: both are necessary components of science and religion."

Bruce Sheiman, An Atheist Defends Religion

The evidence: God provides evidence for his actions

"It is the glory of God to conceal things, but the glory of kings is to search things out."

Proverbs 25:2 ESV

Science as a tool
- Signals of transcendence (Peter Berger)

- Fine tuning of the universe

"The universe and the Laws of Physics seem to have been specifically designed for us. If any one of about forty physical qualities had more than slightly different values, life as we know it could not exist. Either atoms would not be stable or they wouldn't combine into molecules, or the stars wouldn't form heavier elements, or the universe would collapse before life could develop, and so on. . . . The remarkable fact is that the values of these numbers seem to have been very finely adjusted to make possible the development of life."

Stephen Hawking

"Odds of the Big Bang's low entropy condition existing by chance are on the order of one out of $10^{10^{(123)}}$."

Roger Penrose

"A common reaction among physicists to remarkable discoveries is a mixture of delight at the subtlety and elegance of nature, and of stupefaction. If nature is so 'clever' it can exploit mechanisms that amaze us with their ingenuity, is that not persuasive evidence for the existence of intelligent design behind the physical universe?"

Paul Davies

The beginning of the universe

"This newly revealed text was 3 billion letters long, and written in a strange and cryptographic four-letter code. Such is the amazing complexity of the information carried within each cell of the human body, that a live reading of that code at a rate of three letters per second would take thirty-one years, even if reading continued day and night. Printing these letters out in regular font size on normal bond paper and binding them all together would result in a tower of the height of the Washington Monument. For the first time on that summer morning this amazing script, carrying within it all of the instruction for building a human being, was available to the world."

Francis Collins

Evidence of a divine mind

Biomimetics: To look at science through the lens of life

"But ask the beasts, and they will teach you; the birds of the heavens, and they will tell you; or the bushes of the earth, and they will teach you; and the fish of the sea will declare to you. Who among all these does not know that the hand of the LORD has done this?"

Job 12:7–9 ESV

Signals of transcendence

Purposeful design

"For you formed my inward parts; you knitted me together in my mother's womb. I praise you, for I am fearfully and wonderfully made."

Psalm 139:13–14 ESV

"Scripture unveils the poetry behind science. There is no conflict; there's just harmony."

VIDEO REFLECTIONS

1. What stood out to you about this conversation on faith and science? How did the conversation challenge, change, or contribute to your clarity regarding faith and science?

2. When were you first made aware of the supposed conflict between science and faith? What were the circumstances? How did you respond?

"I remember the old 'church versus science' narrative from my elementary school days learning about the Copernican Revolution. We were taught that Christians have been afraid of science because it undermines the church's authority and erodes belief in God. This is an old misconception."

Read: Romans 1:18–23

3. How has God used science to confirm your faith? And how has God used your faith to confirm science?

"The most common misconception about science is that it is the sole means by which we know truth."

Read: Acts 17:24–28

4. Abdu mentioned several limitations and self-defeating beliefs of science: scientism; we are just machines; science and the purpose of humanity; science and morality; science and racial equality. Which limitation of science is the easiest for you to understand or explain? Which limitation is hardest for you to understand or explain?

Read: Hebrews 11:1–3 in ESV, NASB, NRSV, NIV, and KJV translations

5. Abdu refers to *pistis,* the Greek translation of the word *faith*, which literally means "trust." What activities or beliefs in your life require you to have faith? Which activities are actually worthy of your faith?

The Bible doesn't define faith as belief without evidence, but rather faith is trust based on evidence. Have you ever applied the wrong understanding of faith in your life or communicated this misunderstanding to a non-Christian? What happened?

"Blaise Pascal said that God has provided enough evidence in this world to make belief in him quite reasonable, but he has withheld enough evidence to make belief in him without faith impossible."

Read: Proverbs 25:2

6. Abdu reminds us that God delights in our discoveries. Name a time when you watched a child, friend, coworker, teammate, or classmate pursue something with a sense of wonder. What discoveries, inquiries, or searches have created a sense of wonder in your own life?

"Only now, with our high-powered microscopes, are we able to see the engineering marvels all around us that were once hidden from our view. Once again, God in his glory has concealed things so that we can delight in finding them."

Read: Job 12:7–12

7. How does our sense of wonder reflect the image of God, faithfully and scientifically?

Read: Psalm 139:13–14

8. You were intimately designed by the God of the universe. What does that say about you? What does this make you think or how does this make you feel?

"When coupled with a larger worldview that allows for nature's design to speak to us about ultimate purpose, science can lead us to see that we are significant and relevant not only to each other but also to the One who created it all."

CLOSING PRAYER PROMPTS

- Thank God for the faith he's given you to trust in him.
- Give God praise for clarity provided in the Bible regarding the scientific and artistic design of the world.
- Ask God to deepen your understanding of how faith and science weave together as he prepares your heart and mind for conversations regarding the confusion and clarity of our post-truth culture.
- Ask God to renew your sense of wonder in the world around you—the people in your life, the work you get to do, the beauty of nature in your area.
- Thank God for the ways he has intimately designed you and the world around you. Allow yourself to be still and experience a sense of gratitude for God's creativity.

Between Sessions

PERSONAL REFLECTION

Take time to think and journal about the following questions.

"We use reason to infer that the cause of what is visible is invisible. We see the evidence of the physical world around us, and this allows us to reasonably infer that it must have come from a non-physical, unseeable source. And it is by faith—trust—that we understand God to be that source."

What is hard or easy about faith for you? Which relationship, belief, or activity requires the most amount of faith in your life? How does your faith in God influence your faith in the world around you (relationships, beliefs, activities, and so on)?

God has orchestrated the universe and our existence to foster a sense of wonder. And the fact that God hasn't spoon-fed us all the answers reveals something wonderful about his character. He gives us the pleasure of pursuing our wonder through discovering things that are not so obvious. How does this ring true for you? What "newness" have you discovered with your sense of wonder? If you're struggling to think of an answer, then consider what holds you back from experiencing a sense of wonder. What specific steps can you take to be more mindful of staying open to your God-given sense of wonder?

We briefly talked about biomimetics in this session as "looking at science through the lens of life and allowing nature to instruct us on how to make things." In the book, *Saving Truth*, Abdu describes biomimetics as "the science of solving human engineering problems by mimicking the structures and functions of biological organisms." Take a look around you. How have you practiced this "bioinspiration" concept by mimicking the structures and functions of nature in the way you lead, create, decorate, structure, or design your world?

PERSONAL PRAYER JOURNEY

Use a separate journal or the space provided here.

- Journal prayers for friends who need clarity regarding the intersection of faith and science. Ask God to reveal himself to these friends through you—your relationship with God and your sense of wonder regarding the world.

DIGGING DEEPER

Understanding the Science of Faith
Take time to understand how the Christian faith and the findings of science are harmonious. Consider the passages below and how they will help you grow in your faith. Use the space provided to collect your insights and thoughts.

"The late sociologist Peter Berger coined a crystalline-sounding phrase about the small hints in life that point us to God. He called these hints *signals of transcendence*. Although science is a limited tool by which we explore the natural or physical world, what we learn through science has implications for our understanding of the supernatural. In other words, science, when used as a tool for the search for truth, can reveal signals of transcendence."

Read: Job 38:4–30 *(God reminds Job that he is the one who created the world)*
Signals of transcendence found in nature in this passage:

What stands out to me about this passage?

Read: Psalm 136:1–9
Signals of transcendence found in nature in this passage:

What stands out to me about this passage?

Read: Psalm 147:1–11
Signals of transcendence found in nature in this passage:

What stands out to me about this passage?

Read: Psalm 148

Signals of transcendence found in nature in this passage:

What stands out to me about this passage?

The Evidence of a Divine Design

"The Bible doesn't say that we are built, manufactured, or even designed. It describes our creation in a much more intimate way. . . . And the signals of transcendence reveal our relevance to the Transcendent One."

Read: Psalm 139

Name the intimate, delicate, and descriptive details that stand out to you about God's design for you:

-
-
-
-

Because of these specific details of God's divine design in your life, then these things must be true about you:

-
-
-
-

Pray for opportunities to share with someone who needs to know that they have been designed by a God who *loves* them, *knows* them, *sees* them, *understands* them, and *hears* them. And may you wear the coat of Jesus well as you express his transcendent love to the people in your sphere of influence.

DEEPER LEARNING

As you reflect on what God is teaching you through this session, you may want to read chapter 7 of the book *Saving Truth: Finding Meaning and Clarity in a Post-Truth World*. In preparation for your next session, you might want to read chapter 8 of the book.

JOURNAL, REFLECTIONS, AND NOTES

_____
_____
_____
_____
_____
_____
_____
_____
_____
_____
_____
_____
_____
_____
_____

Clarity about Religious Pluralism

Pluralism was once a clear idea. It meant that all religious and nonreligious worldviews were welcome to set up their booths in the marketplace of ideas where we could debate their merits. Today, pluralism is an amorphous concept that confusingly uses "tolerance" to shield certain religions from scrutiny and assail other religions for having the temerity of believing that they're actually true. Failure to recognize that all religious views are exclusive at some level is at the heart of the culture's confusion about religious pluralism today. Recovering clarity about pluralism is critical if we're to truly understand and respect each other.

INTRODUCTION

In the Name of Tolerance

Pluralism is a good thing, and religious pluralism is especially good. It allows us to explore different claims about the most important questions in life, like purpose, meaning, and destiny. We used to be able to explore these claims in what Os Guinness calls the Civil Public Square. The problem today is that the public square isn't always very civil.

In the past few decades, our religious rhetoric had become so heated that all we ever seemed to do is inflame each other's anger. We grew weary of the vitriol, so society underwent a pendular swing. To avoid hurting anyone's feelings, we decided that we can no longer scrutinize anyone's religious claims (well, almost anyone's).

Accordingly, we've shunned almost all religious debate. When someone makes a religious claim, we can't ask probing questions. We have to smile and nod with interest, lest we be branded intolerant. The cost of avoiding that stigma has been ignorance about the richness of the various religious traditions. That self-imposed ignorance gives birth to a confusion with many heads.

We confuse engaging in argumentation with quarreling. We confuse disagreeing with someone's beliefs with disrespecting the person. In fact, we've confused the difference between people and ideas altogether. Where we once used to be able to challenge a person's beliefs without necessarily denigrating that person, we now think that challenging certain beliefs is the same thing as denigrating the person who holds them.

This is especially puzzling because we don't seem to hold back on criticism in other areas of life. No one is arguing that differing economic and political systems are essentially the same. So why are we doing this with religion?

We use easily identifiable and comforting mantras to describe our religious tolerance in the Culture of Confusion, mantras such as, "There are many paths up the spiritual mountain," and, "All roads lead to God." The sentiments of mutual respect that underlie these mantras is well-meaning enough. But their simplistic gloss does exactly the opposite of what they intend. Rather than express a deep understanding of world religions, today's popular mantras convey flippancy and disrespect for them.

When we can no longer have conversations about religious pluralism in the public square because of anger, incivility, and tolerant intolerance, it's as if the Culture of Confusion is carelessly waving tolerance around like a toddler who's found his father's gun. Confusion about whether any particular religion is true has become a virtue. And clarity about the differences in religion—and that they can't all be right—has become a vice. Personal preferences have dominated facts and truth yet again.

Recovering clarity about pluralism is critical if we're to truly understand and respect each other. This session offers clarity that tolerance simply can't mean universal agreement with everyone's different beliefs. In fact, only by recognizing fundamental disagreements can we take different faith systems seriously and respectfully. And it's worth investigating the claim that Jesus is the only way to God.

THINK ABOUT IT

Have you ever had a civil disagreement with a friend, coworker, classmate, or family member? What topic were you discussing? How did the conversation go?

-or-

In what ways have you experienced religious pluralism in your own life or in our society?

VIDEO TEACHING NOTES

Clarity about religious pluralism: What is religious pluralism?

The problem
- Spiritual relativism: Differences exist, but they are personal

- Spiritual syncretism: Manufacturing agreement between worldviews by smoothing over the differences

"No one argues that different economic systems or political regimes are one and the same. Capitalism and socialism are so obviously at odds that their differences hardly bear mentioning. The same goes for democracy and monarchy. Yet scholars continue to claim that religious rivals such as Hinduism and Islam, Judaism and Christianity are, by some miracle of the imagination, essentially the same."

Stephen Prothero, God Is Not One

Tolerance: Confusion is tolerance, and clarity is intolerant

"All roads lead to God."

Popular spiritual mantra

Disrespecting religious claims
- Islam

- Hinduism

- Buddhism

Respecting religious claims: The dignity of difference
- Muslims

- Christians

Tolerance implies differences, not sameness

"Contrast is the mother of clarity."

Os Guinness

The existence of God

"There is no proof for the existence or the nonexistence of God and anyone who tells you otherwise is trying to convert you. Faith is a choice. But it's not an irrational choice. It is the result of one's empirical experience of the world, and of reality, and one's place in the world. You either believe that there is something beyond the material realm or you don't. And you can't be convinced, one way or the other."

Reza Aslan

The post-truth mindset: The preference that all religions are equal has overtaken truth

Inclusivists vs. Exclusivists

"The ideal of religious tolerance has morphed into the straitjacket of religious agreement."

Stephen Prothero

Exclusive truth: The gospel truth is exclusive because truth is exclusive by definition
- Buddhism:

"But the most astonishing thing about Buddhism, and perhaps its greatest contribution to the conversation among the great religions, is its teaching that the thing we are most certain of—the self—is actually a figment of the imagination. Descartes said, 'I think, therefore I am.' Buddhists say if you think carefully enough, you will see that you are not. According to Buddhists, the self (Cartesian or otherwise) does not actually exist."

Stephen Prothero

- Hinduism:

"The Hindu goal, therefore, is not to escape from this world to some heavenly paradise, but to escape from heaven and earth altogether. In Hindu temples and scriptures, we are miles away from the transcendent God of Judaism, Christianity, and Islam, who may have desires but is a stranger to need. Hindu deities are more like us. In this tradition, human beings need the gods, and the gods need human beings."

Stephen Prothero

- Islam:

In Islam, it is blasphemous to say:
- God is personally knowable
- God has a Son
- God is triune

- Confucianism:

"Confucianism distinguishes itself from many other religions by its lack of interest in the divine."

Stephen Prothero

They can't all be right; they have to be different if we are to take them seriously

Jesus as the exclusive truth

"Jesus answered, 'I am the way and the truth and the life. No one comes to the Father except through me.'"

John 14:6 NIV

"And there is salvation in no one else, for there is no other name under heaven given among men by which we must be saved."

Acts 4:12 ESV

Why should we take Jesus seriously?

Religious commonalities: There is a danger in only focusing on our differences

The Qur'an says that if God were to judge humanity according to what it deserves, the whole world would be destroyed.

Sura 35:45

"What the world's religions share is not so much a finish line as a starting point. And where they begin is with this simple observation: something is wrong with the world."

Stephen Prothero

The commonality of human effort: All non-Christian views share one aspect of the finish line regarding human effort

- Pantheism:

- Atheism:

- Hinduism:

- Islam:

- Confucianism:

"Confucians have always had a faith, bordering on fanaticism, in the ability of human beings to improve and even perfect themselves."

Stephen Prothero

- Buddhism:

- Judaism:

There is a commonality to this: We are the problem. And though we are the problem, we are also the solution.

The contrast of the gospel: We need a Savior

The convergence in claiming Jesus

Our recognition

To Narayana: "Thy name will carry me over the sea of this world, Thou dost run to help the distressed, Now run to me, Narayana, to me, poor and wretched as I am. Consider neither my merit nor my faults. Tukaram implores thy mercy."

Tukaram

The gospel's distinctive: An informed choice and a verifiable faith

"For God so loved the world that He gave His only begotten Son, that whoever believes in Him should not perish but have everlasting life."

John 3:16 NKJV

The cross of Jesus is the exclusive means of salvation, but everyone is invited to trust in him

VIDEO REFLECTIONS

1. What stood out to you about this conversation on religious pluralism? How did this conversation challenge, change, or contribute to your clarity regarding religious pluralism?

2. How has studying other religions strengthened your faith? Or what negative effect has it had on your faith?

3. Abdu mentions a shift in our culture as civil conversations have morphed into conversations about universal agreement and inclusivity. How have you specifically noticed this cultural shift?

"Recognizing and honestly wrestling with these diverse claims affords religious people the dignity of difference. If we don't acknowledge the fundamental differences, we end up disrespecting thousands of years of each religion's traditions and theological development."

Read: Acts 4:10–12

4. How would you summarize the commonalities shared by various religious traditions? How would you summarize the differences among these religious traditions?

"Observing differences and similarities among worldviews helps us to gain clarity on the answers to life's most important questions. Our common recognition that the world is in need of fixing serves as the platform from which we can see which of the different pools that offer solutions are worth jumping into."

Read: John 14:1–7

5. Do you believe Jesus is the exclusive truth? Why or why not?

"Where other religious founders claimed to *have* the truth, Jesus claims to *be* the way and the truth. . . . His audacious claim to *be* the way and truth is substantiated by objective proof."

Read: Matthew 16:13–23

6. How have we, as Christians, contributed to the confusion or done a disservice with our attitudes regarding the exclusive truth of Jesus?

"Our Culture of Confusion—which tries to make all religions equal and rob Christ of his cross—is strikingly similar to Peter. We admire Jesus so much, yet we tailor him to fit our preferred worldviews. In so doing, we are very much like another of Jesus' disciples, Judas, who betrayed Jesus with a kiss."

Read: James 2:14–17

7. How does the idea of human effort appear in different religious traditions? How does the idea of human effort appear in our Christian traditions today? As Christians, how should our efforts interact with our faith?

Read: John 3:16–18

8. Abdu describes the gospel as exclusive truth because he says it is an *informed choice* and a *verifiable faith*. Now imagine a day when we can return to thoughtful conversations in the public square. When given the opportunity to share your faith, what reasons would you give as to why your faith is an informed, verifiable choice?

"The Christian message is that there is an exclusive way to get to God. And that one way cost God more than it will ever cost us. But the invitation to accept it includes us all."

CLOSING PRAYER PROMPTS

- Thank God for the perspective and truth he's given you through Jesus.
- Give God praise for the gift of salvation and his invitation and love for everyone.
- Ask God to give you a sense of the dignity of people around you who practice and participate in different religious beliefs.
- Ask God to deepen your understanding of different religious beliefs and the claims they make regarding truth, so that you are equipped with wisdom and seasoned with grace in your conversations.
- Thank God for evidence of Jesus that gives us the freedom to choose to believe in him based on information, not preferences.

Between Sessions

PERSONAL REFLECTION

Take time to think and journal about the following questions.

"Jesus gave us verifiable evidence that he is God incarnate who came to this earth to give his life in payment for our transgressions. That evidence gives us the freedom to choose to believe in him, based not on chaotic emotional preferences, but on information. Only an informed choice is a meaningful choice."

Why do you think God allows other religious traditions to exist? And why does God give us the *choice* to choose him or believe in something or someone else?

If our meaningful choices are informed choices, as Abdu Murray says in his book *Saving Truth*, then what meaningful choices have you made recently? Take note of even the small meaningful choices you've made. Now think back over your life as a whole. What meaningful and informed choices have made the greatest difference in your life?

In his closing statements for this session, Abdu said, "The informed choice is that Jesus gave us the proof of his resurrection. He loves everyone and invites anyone. The cross of Jesus is the exclusive means of salvation, but everyone is invited to trust in him." By giving us the choice to accept or reject him as the exclusive truth, Jesus' invitation welcomes all of us and embraces everything we carry with us—our knowledge, our experiences, our doubt, our trust, and our love. What made you accept the invitation of Jesus? How did accepting this invitation make a difference in your life? How did it change your perspective on religious pluralism? Or, if you haven't accepted the invitation of Jesus, what's keeping you from his invitation? What's holding you back at this point?

PERSONAL PRAYER JOURNEY

Use a separate journal or the space provided here.

- Journal prayers for friends who need clarity regarding religious pluralism, civil conversations, and the exclusive truth of Jesus. Ask God to reveal himself to these friends through you or directly, addressing their questions, doubts, or fears of acknowledging the truth and resurrection of Jesus.

DIGGING DEEPER

Confusion and the Roads to God

Take time to explore the various religious traditions mentioned in this session and understand the main differences in their tenets of faith. Revisit your video notes, listen to the teaching again, or do some reputable reading on your own. Use the space provided to collect your insights and thoughts.

"Different religious beliefs cause us to put our own beliefs to the test. That's true tolerance. And tolerance can lead to clarity."

Name the main points of these religious traditions and note the differences between them and other traditions:

Islam:
-
-
-

Hinduism:
-
-
-

Buddhism:
-
-
-

Confucianism:
-
-
-

Christianity:

-
-
-

The Evidence of Exclusive Truth

Take time to understand what Scripture has to say about the exclusive truth of Jesus. Consider the passages below and how they will help you grow in your faith. Use the space provided to collect your insights and thoughts.

"If we confuse universal agreement with tolerance, we end up indicting every single religious (or even nonreligious) view as intolerant. This is why Jesus' claim to be the sole means of salvation doesn't put him outside the realm of tolerance, but squarely within it. Jesus' claim is quite unequivocal."

Read: Acts 4:1–22

Claims of exclusive truth found in this passage:

What stands out to me about this passage?

Read: Romans 10:9–13

Claims of exclusive truth found in this passage:

What stands out to me about this passage?

Read: James 2:14–16

Claims of exclusive truth found in this passage:

What stands out to me about this passage?

Read: John 3:16–21

Claims of exclusive truth found in this passage:

What stands out to me about this passage?

Read: James 3

Claims of exclusive truth found in this passage:

What stands out to me about this passage?

Pray for opportunities to share the invitation of Jesus and his resurrection as proof of the exclusive truth. And may you walk in the love of Jesus as you have conversations regarding religious pluralism, tolerance, confusion, and clarity in our post-truth world.

DEEPER LEARNING

As you reflect on what God is teaching you through this session, you may want to read chapter 8 of the book *Saving Truth: Finding Meaning and Clarity in a Post-Truth World*. In preparation for your next session, you might want to read chapter 9 of the book.

JOURNAL, REFLECTIONS, AND NOTES

The Son through Fog: Clarity's Hope

Hope. It's the feeling or desire that things will work out for the best. We hope for things to work out because we are uncertain that they will. In other worlds, we often hope because we are unsure. We weaken our grip on hope by celebrating confusion as virtuous while decrying clarity as sinful. But our grasp on hope can be strengthened if we reorient our wistful gaze from the foggy unsure to the clear. The Son shines through the fog giving us the light to find hope in the post-truth Culture of Confusion.

INTRODUCTION

The Clarity of Hope

The controversial issues of our day act like fault lines that erode the bedrock of clarity. Controversy arises, quite literally, when we turn against something or someone. We think of controversies most often as a public debate over opposing views, and indeed controversy has flourished in our day when autonomy is the ultimate goal. When our individual autonomies collide, the inevitable result will be to turn against each other.

But controversy's deepest fissures aren't public. They're private.

One may champion unrestrained freedom yet subconsciously recognize that true freedom must be bound by truth. A person may want to define his or her own sexual and gender identity only to find that fulfillment remains elusive. We try to limit our worldview to what science can measure, but then stare at the horizon wondering if there's more to life than this mortal coil. Our preferences have not given us the sure footing of clarity's dry land, only the wobbling buoyancy of confusion's river.

These internal controversies—not the public ones—make the gospel's simple clarity appealing yet difficult to embrace. And the gospel really is simple. It is the good news that you and I are sinners in need of a savior and Jesus is that Savior. Because of what God has done in the past, we can have faith in what he will do in our futures.

But we still ask—can something so simple be all-encompassing? How can one idea—indeed one person, Jesus—clarify our culture's confusion and bring us the clarity we need? Indeed, to say that the gospel is simple yet all-encompassing seems contradictory, but it isn't. In fact, it's our fragmentation of life that's too small to handle this world. We see no overarching, simple idea that connects all our fragmented views.

We're so obsessed over the freedom to do what we want that we've neglected the freedom to do what we should. To wrap our minds around what it means to be human, we've focused narrowly on brain chemistry, thereby reducing ourselves to freedomless chemical machines. This in turn leads us to contradictorily conclude that with regard to sexual and gender identity, we're "born that way" but should be allowed to explore as many sexual or gender expressions as we want. We give lip service to respecting all religions only to turn against a particular religion if it doesn't line up with our irreligious autonomy. Life is complicated and we need nuanced answers to life's questions.

A stained-glass window is complex too. But the outer frame that holds its intricate pieces

140

together is usually a simple square or circle. We must embrace this paradox to find clarity: the comprehensive answers to life's complicated questions emanate from one straightforward worldview. We can become convinced that one worldview, a simple idea, offers hope because it corrals all of life's complexities. Life's innumerable complexities are marshaled under the hope of one clarity: we are made in the image of God.

So, *what is truth?* We may ask this question in a world that elevates personal preference over truth. The answer is Jesus—the truth who is personal. He is the Saving Truth.

THINK ABOUT IT

Have you ever felt hopeless? Why did you feel that way? What eventually brought hope to your hopeless situation?

-or-

What gives you hope today? And what causes you to be hopeful about tomorrow?

VIDEO TEACHING NOTES

The clarity of the gospel: Hope

Hope allows us to endure the pain and uncertainty of life

The celebration of confusion: Hope weakens when we celebrate confusion
- What is freedom?
- What does it mean to be human?
- Are gender and sexuality sacred or can we make it whatever we want it to be?
- Is faith in God blind or can we back it up with science?
- Can there really be only one way to God?

Saving truth from a post-truth culture

The hope we need: Can the gospel give us answers and hope?

The gospel's framework: Holding the complex ideas of life together

"If we live as Christians, we will be wiser and more aware of the dangers we face. We will not separate morality from truth. We will not confuse moral autonomy with any free choice. We will not treat individuals, whether the unborn or the dying, as things. We will not allow all desires to be transformed into rights. We will not confine reason within the boundaries of science. Nor will we feel alone in a society of strangers or oppressed by the state that appropriates us because we no longer know how to guide ourselves."

Marcello Pera, atheist

Faith, hope, and love

"So now faith, hope, and love abide, these three; but the greatest of these is love."

1 Corinthians 13:13 ESV

The power of truth to bring hope
- **Question:** Why would God create a world that would devolve into a Culture of Confusion?
- **Answer:** The answer reveals the character of a God worth believing in, which can give us hope

God created us so we can have relationship

"Precious in the sight of the Lord is the death of his saints."

Psalm 116:15 ESV

"Say to them, As I live, declares the Lord God, I have no pleasure in the death of the wicked, but that the wicked turn from his way and live; turn back, turn back from your evil ways, for why will you die, O house of Israel?"

Ezekiel 33:11 ESV

Our limited vulnerability: We can choose who we love

God's unlimited love: God feels the pain of rejection
- **Question:** Why would God create humans, knowing we would cause him pain?
- **Answer:** God creates us with real choice because of his selfless character

Finding hope and fulfillment in our post-truth culture

How can the resurrection of Jesus lead to truth and freedom?

The resurrection as proof: Jesus paid our debt

We know the value of things by what we're willing to pay for them

"So Jesus said to the Jews who had believed him, 'If you abide in my word, you are truly my disciples, and you will know the truth, and the truth will set you free.'"

John 8:31–32 ESV

Truth is not only personal, it is a person. And he is the Saving Truth.

VIDEO REFLECTIONS

1. What stood out to you about this conversation on finding hope and saving truth? How did this conversation challenge, change, or contribute to your clarity regarding living out your faith in our post-truth culture?

2. Of all the questions asked by our post-truth culture in the midst of confusion, which one is still the biggest question for you: freedom, human value, gender and sexual identity, science and faith, or the idea of one way to God?

Read: 1 Corinthians 15:54–58

3. How has hope allowed you to endure the pain and uncertainty of life?

"Because of what God has done in the past, we can have faith in what he will do in our futures. Secular hope is uncertain. Biblical hope is sure."

Read: 1 Corinthians 13:11–13

4. Do you truly believe the gospel gives us the answers and the hope we need? Why or why not? How have you personally found answers and hope in the message of the gospel?

"In short, everything 'proves' the gospel and the gospel 'proves' everything. With such clarity, our fingers wrap tighter around a sure hope for a better future."

Read: Joshua 24:15; John 7:17

5. How do you explain the freedom God gives us in our relationship with him? Has there ever been a time when you exercised your freedom to reject God? Or accept him?

"We aren't meant to be puppets dancing as God's marionettes. We are created to have fulfilling, everlasting intimacy with God. That relationship entails the freedom to embrace or reject God."

Read: Psalm 34:18; Psalm 116:15; Ezekiel 33:11

6. How have we contributed to God's pain as humans living in a post-truth culture?

"We often think of rejection's consequences as one-sided: we reject God and we suffer for it. But that ignores a fundamental truth: our rejection affects God as well. To God, we are immeasurably valuable whether we embrace or reject him."

Read: 1 Timothy 2:5–6

7. Abdu says, "We know the value of things by what we're willing to pay for them." How is this illustrated in your own life or in our culture? What do we "say" we value according to the prices we're willing to pay?

Read: John 8:31–36

8. How has Jesus been the Saving Truth in your life? Understanding Jesus as our Saving Truth, how has this study changed your perspective on the way you interact with the post-truth world in which we live?

"We don't need something to make us alive. We need someone. . . . Clarity will return most fully when we see the gospel for what it is and see Jesus for who he is."

CLOSING PRAYER PROMPTS

- Thank God for the clarity and truth he's given us through his Son, Jesus.
- Give God praise for the fact that the complexity of human life is summarized under one source of clarity—that we were made in the image of God.
- Ask God to give you a sense of confidence as you speak with clarity regarding his truth.
- Ask God to deepen your experience of his truth as your guide while navigating the post-truth Culture of Confusion. And ask God to reveal any of your mindsets or beliefs that need to be realigned to his truth.
- Thank God for the freedom he gives us to embrace or reject him. Thank him for the personal gift he offers each one of us to enter into a loving relationship with Jesus as our Savior and as the God of the universe.

In the Coming Days

PERSONAL REFLECTION

Take time to think and journal about the following questions.

"And this is eternal life, that they know you, the only true God, and Jesus Christ whom you have sent."

John 17:3 ESV

Abdu cleared up a lot of confusion regarding our post-truth mindset by talking through specific areas of cultural confusion and ultimately clarifying that Jesus is the person who saves all truth. How does Jesus specifically provide clarity for you in your personal life? How does he provide clarity as you look at the culture around you?

Is there an area of your life that needs to be cleared up, cleaned out, or surrendered in order for you to live a life consistent with God's truth? What steps will you take to move toward clarity and away from confusion in this area? Who can hold you accountable and encourage you as you take these steps?

The moment of truth: If you have not decided to put your faith and trust in Jesus, would you consider doing so now? Are you willing to say yes to a life of clarity and truth in Jesus? *If so, take a few minutes to pray and ask Jesus to be the one true God in your life, and thank him for the gift of freedom and salvation you now accept because of his death and resurrection.* Or maybe you trusted Jesus with your life a long time ago, but you've turned away or rejected him as your source of truth. *If this is you and you long to be in relationship with him, then ask Jesus for forgiveness and thank him for the freedom to choose him all over again.*

PERSONAL PRAYER JOURNEY

Use a separate journal or the space provided here.

- Journal prayers for yourself as you walk in the clarity of the truth of Jesus, and for your friends who need to be rescued from the confusion of the post-truth mindset. Ask God for opportunities to share his truth, his light, and his love in the midst of the confusion around you.

DIGGING DEEPER

Jesus Is Our Saving Truth

Take time to review what Scripture has to say about Jesus as our Saving Truth. Consider the passages below and how they will help you grow in your faith. Use the space provided to collect your insights and thoughts.

"In Jesus Christ, we have both the truth who satisfies our quest and the personality who satisfies our need for connection. He is the truth our minds seek and the person our hearts embrace. He validates facts and personal preferences without sacrificing either."

Read: John 8

As our Saving Truth, Jesus gives us:

What stands out to me about this passage?

Read: 1 Corinthians 13

As our Saving Truth, Jesus gives us:

What stands out to me about this passage?

Read: Galatians 5

As our Saving Truth, Jesus gives us:

What stands out to me about this passage?

Read: Romans 10

As our Saving Truth, Jesus gives us:

What stands out to me about this passage?

Read: John 14

As our Saving Truth, Jesus gives us:

What stands out to me about this passage?

The Hope of Clarity

Take time to review the areas of cultural confusion identified in our post-truth world, and write down a few points of clarity you gained from this study. Revisit your video notes and use the space provided to collect your insights and thoughts.

"Jesus secures humanity's freedom to be what we were intended to be: sacred beings in relationship with the divine. When we realize that, confusion dissipates like fog and clarity remains."

Freedom:

-
-

Human dignity:

-
-

Sexuality, gender, and identity:

-
-

Science and faith:

-
-

Religious pluralism:

-
-

Jesus as our Saving Truth:

-
-

Pray for opportunities to share the clarity you've gained as a result of this study. And pray for opportunities to bring the hope of clarity to the confusion of a post-truth world as you interact with friends, family members, colleagues, classmates, and teammates.

DEEPER LEARNING

As you reflect on what God is teaching you through this session, you may want to read chapter 9 of the book *Saving Truth: Finding Meaning and Clarity in a Post-Truth World*. If you are interested in learning more from Abdu Murray, consider reading his previous book, *Grand Central Question: Answering the Critical Concerns of the Major Worldviews*.

JOURNAL, REFLECTIONS, AND NOTES

Closing Words

Let me end by saying this: the gospel message is clear that we are all sinners, utterly undeserving of God's grace and mercy. We owe God a debt and are unable to pay it. Jesus paid that debt for us. Being fully God and fully human, Jesus was able to live a perfect life so that he had no sins of his own to pay for and could hang on that cross as our representative.

The fact of our sin ought to squash any sense of pride in us. The fact that Jesus offered himself as payment for us ought to dismantle any prideful sense in us that the gospel is true because it is *ours*. Jesus didn't claim to be my truth, my way, and my life. He claimed to be *the* way, *the* truth, and *the* life. He isn't the exclusive Savior because he saved me. He's the exclusive Savior—the Lamb of God—who takes away the sins of the world.

When both Christians and non-Christians see this, perhaps both will see the exclusive claims of Christ and his sacrifice for our sins not as the "secret password" that gains us entry into a special club, but as the humble actions of a Most High God offered to each one of us. And lest we be confused on which group of people these exclusive claims are for, the most famous passage of the Bible gives us clarity. In John 3:16 we read, "For God so loved *the world*"—that's everyone—"that he gave his one and only Son, that *whoever* believes in him"—that's anyone—"shall not perish but have eternal life" (NIV, emphasis added).

The invitation to step out of confusion and into clarity through the exclusive, saving truth of Jesus is open to all. My hope for each one of you as you finish this study is that you have regained clarity regarding the deepest questions in our Culture of Confusion, and that you know and accept Jesus as the Saving Truth.

Thank you for joining me for *Saving Truth: Finding Meaning and Clarity in a Post-Truth World*. It has been a joy to walk alongside each one of you on your quest for clarity. May you live a life of purpose, meaning, and dignity as you wear the coat of Jesus well in the world around you.

Abdu Murray